LOVE AND TREASON.

𝔄 𝔑𝔬𝔳𝔢𝔩.

By WILLIAM FREELAND.

IN THREE VOLUMES.
VOL. III.

LONDON:

TINSLEY BROTHERS, 18 CATHERINE ST. STRAND.

1872.

CONTENTS OF VOL. III.

vi

LOVE AND TREASON.

CHAPTER I.

LOCHABER NO MORE.

It was the end of September, a fine day. The sun looked as if he had risen that morning for the first time, and for some special purpose; his face was so cloudless, and his beam so mellow.

At the Broomielaw lay the ship Columbia, laden with Glasgow merchandise for New York. A goodly ship she was, and Captain MacTavish was a goodly commander. Tall, red-haired, and red-whiskered, with eyes that gleamed steadily under strong eyebrows, and with cheek-bones and temples scorched and corrugated by Mediterranean suns and Atlantic tempests, he stood or walked on the deck like a veritable sea-king.

It was the afternoon; and as the solar fire-flood poured unimpeded into the harbour, which was peopled with prophetic motions and murmurs of the far-off sea, the Clyde flashed and sparkled like a river of weltering gold. Everything was steeped in the yellow sunlight; and the very ships, from hull to topgallant, looked as if they also were built of gold. A few gulls glided lazily and liquidly up and down the harbour, and they too seemed winged with gold. The very garbage which they picked from the water glittered for a moment like golden food —and to the gulls, no doubt, it was a very delicious feast.

Even at that time the harbour of Glasgow was a peculiarly busy scene, and it had begun to manifest symptoms of that marvellous commercial vitality which now throbs along its masted miles. On this glorious September day a large number of vessels, of various nationalities, were moored at the quays, all in process either of being laden with home manu- factures or unladen of foreign produce — sugar, tea, tobacco, cotton, and all kinds of odorous spiceries. Strange voices were heard among the sailors; and by walking along on either side of the harbour one could hear tongues babble in many human languages.

Among the ships which were getting ready for clearing out, the Columbia was the most advanced. Indeed, Captain MacTavish looked as if he could have cleared out that very moment. But he could not legally do so for half an hour; and the emigrants who were about to sail with him for the New World lingered on Scottish soil as long as possible. They were inhaling farewell breaths of the free, historic air of their native land and language, mingled in some instances with occasional consolatory draughts of pure mountain dew. In other cases, the emigrants, especially the females, were assailed with choking emotions in having to leave the sacred soil of home. The splendour of the day only deepened the sorrow, for it made home so beautiful. Had it been foggy, rainy, or dirty weather of some kind, the step from the harbour to the ship would have been greatly facilitated. But as it was, the poor emigrants moved towards the edge of the river by half inches, and each half inch was a pang like the breaking of a heart. They knew they must go; but they seemed unwilling to go; and friends clung to them, and would not let them go. The hard stones of the quay were wet with women's tears.

But, of course, some were less profoundly affected. Over those who are born citizens of the world the tender associations of home have little power; and there is a species of men who regard themselves as being wronged and insulted because they are born on the soil of their forefathers. To such men any land is better than their own, and therefore they make the most willing emigrants. Two or three of these oddities were about to sail

in the Columbia for America; and as they stood on
the shore chattering with their acquaintances, they
rather wondered than otherwise why Captain Mac-
Tavish delayed so long. One of them was Jock
Makane.

'Ye needna wonner ony mair, Pate,' said Jock
to his old friend, the twister, who had come to see
him aboard; 'ye've kent my sentiments for a gay
wheen years, and I'm owre auld in the horn to
change them now. This is no the puir man's country — thanks to your freens, the aristocrats,' and
Jock whispered in Pate's ear—' a Government that
deserved nae better fate than to hae twa-three kegs
o' gunpoother put below their seats, wi' some dry
shavins and a red-het poker, to blaw their rotten
politics and souls to bits !'

'Ye ken the proverb, Jock? "It's an ill bird
that fyles its ain nest." '

'But I dinna ca' this country my nest. It's aye
been a dry nurse and a step-mither to me.'

'True, Jock; and ye've been but a middlin step-
bairn to her. I'm thinkin that ilk country is guid
or bad just as it's weel or ill ta'en or done by; and
ye'll maybe come to see that when ye reach the
country o' Geordie Washington. Ye'll hae ae thing
there in your favour, though—'

'What's that?'

'Plenty o' room. If ye're no pleased wi' New

York, ye can get for maist naething a hale desert to yoursel—millions o' acres, and no ae aristocrat to trouble ye, except, maybe, an anterin lion, the king o' beasts. However, ye can put a bullet in his wame, and no be hanged for't.'

'Ye're pleased to be faceeshus, Pate. But let me tell ye ance for a', I wad think it as sinfu' to kill a lion as to kill that wonnerfu' Prince Regent o' yours. A lion, though a beast, is aye a king; but though Geordie may become king, he'll never be onything but a beast. I pity Great Britain!'

'I ken weel, Jock,' said Pate, 'that ye've nae respect for Powers and Principalities; but I doubt that the pity o' ae Glasgow Radical, fleein' frae his country, will hae sma' effect on Gentleman Geordie, or in mendin' the British Constitution. I had some hope, though, that ye micht at least drap ae tear for bonnie Scotland and auld langsyne.'

'Me drap a tear!'

'Weel, weel, nae mair about it; I've been mista'en, and ye're consistent at least in playin' the character o' the "auld saxpence." It's no easy to change ye. But maybe, when you and Bell are sitting at your ain fire-en' in the New Worl', ye'll cast a bit thought back to auld times and auld freens—particularly to ae twister body that ye kent in the British House o' Bondage.'

'Weel, Pate, I may promise that muckle; and

what's mair, I'll aften wonner to mysel how it was
possible that sae hunger't a soul as that same twister
could hae nae sympathy wi' his fellow-twisters-and-
weavers in the cause o' Reform—men that wad hae
poured out their life-bluid on the scaffold for the
richts o' man.'

'Thank ye, Jock,' answered Pate, with a pawky
twinkle; 'I like your plain words weel. Like the
auld pennies, they gie you guid wecht and a guid
grup; and naebody can refuse to tak them back in
payment for debts. This'll be the last time, I doubt,
that you and me will ever see ane anither in this
life; and I wadna just like to pairt wi' ye in a storm,
as we hae sae aften done afore. But for a' that,
Jock, ye maun tak back twa-three o' your ain pennies. Ye seem to think that I should hae been a
Radical because I'm puir.'

'To be sure. Rags and Radicalism should gang
thegither. The puir man that's no a Radical is no
in his richt mind.'

'Yet mony's the decent puir man I hae kent wha
was neither Radical nor Tory.'

'Nor Whig?'

'No, nor Whig either; but a guid stiff Independent, fechtin' for his ain haun.'

'A man o' that kind is neither flesh nor fowl, nor
even guid red herrin'.'

'That may be sae according to the common

pairty lichts, but downricht false in ony common-
sense licht. Politics founded on rags and hunger
are sure to be a mixture o' hauf truths and hale
lees; and the believers in sic systems are nae better
than a wheen 'silly sheep, followin' whaever gangs
first, though it should be a sow or a sumph wi' a
pickle woo stickit owre him to mak' him look as
silly as the puir flock that trot ahint him wi' their
noses at ane anither's tails. I like to see men
thinkin' for themsel's.'

'Do ye, though?' asked Jock, with a touch of
his ancient humour. 'The warst o' you causey philosophers is that ye are sae muckle ta'en up wi'
thinkin' about your ain independence that ye dinna
seem to care a spittle about ony ither body's independence. Your minds are nae doubt fu' o' grand
ideas, as ye ca' them, but whaur are your guid
warks? Ye canna feed puir folk wi' fine thinkin'.'

'Yet it is said, Jock, that man shall not live by
bread alone.'

'Quite true—he needs a drap drink whiles.'

'That's like ye—Jock maun hae his joke.'

'And Pate his pun.'

'Weel,' said the twister, laughing, 'now that
we're equal, let me tell ye that ideas are as usefu'
as actions; and what's better, that there can be nae
great actions without great ideas.'

'Maybe ye're right: but if sae, it only proves

LOVE AND TREASON.

CHAPTER I.

LOCHABER NO MORE.

It was the end of September, a fine day. The sun looked as if he had risen that morning for the first time, and for some special purpose; his face was so cloudless, and his beam so mellow.

At the Broomielaw lay the ship Columbia, laden with Glasgow merchandise for New York. A goodly ship she was, and Captain MacTavish was a goodly commander. Tall, red-haired, and red-whiskered, with eyes that gleamed steadily under strong eyebrows, and with cheek-bones and temples scorched and corrugated by Mediterranean suns and Atlantic tempests, he stood or walked on the deck like a veritable sea-king.

It was the afternoon; and as the solar fire-flood poured unimpeded into the harbour, which was peo-

'We micht baith be better, Jock, and I hope
there'll be a chance for us yet — for you, at least.
Ye're younger than me, and I wish ye every success
in the country ye're gaun to. If ye dinna meddle
wi' politics there's nae fear o' ye.—What's that?'

Pate's question was suggested by a sound of
lamentation. On looking behind them, they saw,
somewhat removed from the rest of the crowd, a
group of persons, some of whom they knew to be
emigrants about to sail with the Columbia. They
were Highland people from Lochaber side, on Loch
Linnhe, though they had been staying with friends
in the city for some weeks, waiting for a ship to the
New World.

Those who have any acquaintance with the Celtic
character will understand that a Highland parting is
anything but a cold, formal affair. Of all the races
who inhabit these islands, the Highlanders cling
most tenaciously to the place of their birth; so that
leaving it, however poor it may be, is with them like
cutting out a portion of their hearts. It almost
seems, indeed, as if the very scantiness and barren-
ness of the soil only the better served to nourish
their affection for it. The lonely or the lovely glen
—its special torrent, its blooming heather, its spec-
tral mists, its eery voices, and its whirling snow
tempests — each and all of them seem to become
part of their blood and brain, and wherever they go

grants who were about to sail with him for the New
World lingered on Scottish soil as long as possible.
They were inhaling farewell breaths of the free,
historic air of their native land and language, mingled in some instances with occasional consolatory
draughts of pure mountain dew. In other cases, the
emigrants, especially the females, were assailed with
choking emotions in having to leave the sacred soil
of home. The splendour of the day only deepened
the sorrow, for it made home so beautiful. Had it
been foggy, rainy, or dirty weather of some kind, the
step from the harbour to the ship would have been
greatly facilitated. But as it was, the poor emigrants moved towards the edge of the river by half
inches, and each half inch was a pang like the
breaking of a heart. They knew they must go ;
but they seemed unwilling to go ; and friends clung
to them, and would not let them go. The hard
stones of the quay were wet with women's tears.

But, of course, some were less profoundly affected. Over those who are born citizens of the
world the tender associations of home have little
power ; and there is a species of men who regard
themselves as being wronged and insulted because
they are born on the soil of their forefathers. To
such men any land is better than their own, and
therefore they make the most willing emigrants.
Two or three of these oddities were about to sail

knows the tragic depth, Ronald spoke to her in a manner which seemed to transform the tortuous syllables of the Gaelic tongue into the language of Italy or Heaven. Alleyne, as she listened to the passionate breathings of her lover, stood like one charmed, in spite of her woe. Now and then she interposed a few fond words of response; but these, like pearly shoals breaking into tenser murmurs the vowelled volume of a gliding river, only served to give a keener tone to the ceaseless current of his tenderness. He was pleading with her to be true, and he would come out to her in a year. In a voice that hardly impressed the air, she promised to be true and to wait his coming. Still, he seemed unsatisfied, and again and again implored her to be true. At this she was no way offended, but again and again softly protested that she would remain faithful.

But the hour was at length about to strike, and the emigrants must get aboard. It was a sad—a passionate moment. The air was full of sighs and farewells. Ronald Macdonald clasped Alleyne Roy in his arms, and, indifferent to audacious eyes, impressed upon her lips the kisses of a year—the coming year of their separation. Pate Fox had wrung the hands of Jock and his wife. Poor Bell! Unlike her husband, she was shaken with anguish at leaving home; and there was no tender female friend there to soothe her departure and bid her God speed.

The Highland family got at last gathered together,
but their getting on board was a heart-breaking process. Their Glasgow friends, with the lover of Alleyne, hung upon them, wept over them, and poured
upon them a torrent of Gaelic more pathetic than a
coronach. At length, however, they struggled to the
deck of the Columbia, the old man bearing on his
right arm his youngest child, and on his left his
bagpipes, which he bore with equal tenderness.

At this moment, Pate Fox got a little surprise.
He was standing beside Ronald Macdonald, looking
at the huddled deck of the ship, when some commotion took place among those who crowded the quay.
Before he had time to inquire the cause of it, he saw
walking on board the Columbia Alan Dalziel and
Christine Dundas. Alan carried a bundle.

' Gude preserve us !' thought Pate, ' are thae twa
gaun to rin awa, or emigrate ?'

But the purpose of the pair was much simpler
than that. Christine had come on one of her mis-
sions of kindliness and mercy. She wished to take
farewell with Bell, Jock's wife ; and the bundle which
Alan carried was a present, consisting of some warm
clothing. The couple were greatly affected by this
unexpected attention. Bell was softened to. tears ;
and even the granite heart of Jock fluttered with
sensations which had long become dim traditions to
it. As Captain MacTavish, who was a bachelor,

looked at Christine, he wondered in his heart whether it would be permissible to cut his cables and carry her off as a prize. But in three minutes they were out of the ship, which immediately moved into the middle of the river, and prepared to bid adieu to the city.

All this time Ronald Macdonald stood on the quay, with his eyes fixed on a single figure that stood on deck watching him. The face of the young Highlander was a picture wherein desire and indecision contended as if in mortal agony. Surely, if ever two beings loved each other, it was Ronald Macdonald and Alleyne Roy.

At length, as the vessel moved down the river, a murmur of farewells, sent from the shore, was answered from the ship, with something like a wail wrung from choking hearts. Still more fearfully worked the face of the Highland lover as he saw his sweetheart borne away on the tide.

But now was seen a strange spectacle. Alan, Christine, and Pate were standing in a group, quite near, and rather pitying the agonised giant. For a moment they turned their eyes to the Columbia, when they heard a voice saying wildly, 'I canna bide! I canna bide!' In looking round, they caught sight of Ronald Macdonald plunging into the river. There was a cry of alarm from the ship and from the shore, but, above all, was heard the scream of Alleyne Roy, who rushed to the vessel's side as if to follow her drowning lover. But suicide was not in the programme of the passionate Macdonald; and in two minutes he stood, dripping, on the deck of the ship, in the arms of Alleyne, declaring that he could not stay behind, and that he would follow her over the world.

Nor was the soft yet daring Celtic rogue unprepared for the emergency; for with a sort of prophetic instinct, before leaving Lochaber he had put in his purse all the money which he had been gathering in prospect of his marriage with Alleyne.

But his poor widowed mother? His younger brother Angus would take care of her; and he himself would even soon send her some help, perhaps even money, to take them both to America.

Slowly, slowly moved the emigrant ship down the Clyde—slowly, slowly, yet with increasing speed. Still, without moving, stood the people on the shore, straining all eyes to catch final glimpses of their departing friends. But at last they were turning away, when they were arrested by a sound which held them as by a magic spell. Duncan Roy was playing on his pipes, and the sounds that floated up the river from the downward moving ship was the wailing melody of 'Lochaber no more.'

Christine Dundas leaned on Alan's shoulder, silent, thrilled by the music, that seemed to issue from

sobbing, breaking, dying hearts, borne into lands
from which is no returning.

CHAPTER II.

MORE MISCHIEF.

NOTHING is so remarkable as the folly of wise,
the stupidity of clever men—the blindness of those
that see, the dulness of those that understand, and
the lameness of the strong limbed.

These profound reflections are not unwarranted
in authentic history, and they are far more than war-
ranted in the domain of fiction.

We have seen, for instance, how Richmond, infallible in his own conceit, was so crushingly unde-
ceived. He performed the actual work of a spy, believing that he was doing the work of a patriot—not
a fiery, but a cool, statesmanlike patriot—and pre-
suming that he could conceal his operations from the
vulgar, he expected some splendid recognition from
the great—from the Government itself. In effect, he
only succeeded in drawing upon himself the incur-
able scorn and detestation of the class to which he
belonged.

Next, contemplate the Government. Taking its

own measure of itself, no more perfect Government
had ever wielded the destinies of Great Britain. In
the estimation of its enemies, it was the most brutal
and unconciliatory Government which ever disgraced
the annals of the country. The truth, as some
thought, lay between these extremes. The Government was strong, but not wise. It was described as
low-thoughted, and therefore high-handed. It paid
no heed to the petitions for Reform and Retrench-
ment. Yet notwithstanding their failure to gain the
confidence of the country, the Government continued
to repeat itself, turning ears of stone to the voice of
the people, who became in 1820 even more discon-
tented and menacing than in 1817.

Then, look at Alan Dalziel. For a youth wearing
such clear signs of ability, he became early the per-
petrator of many stupidities. Beginning with a fair
prospect of working his way in a good profession, he
ruined himself by making experiments in treason.
But worse still, untaught by that failure, as well as
by many volumes of advice, he permitted himself to
be drawn into the political whirlpool of 1820. Shortly
after his return to the city in 1817, Dr. Bannatyne,
whom he met one night at Cockmylane, suggested
that he should study for the medical profession. The
idea captivated his fancy. He consulted Mr. Dundas
and Christine on the subject, who thought the proposition not only commendable, but feasible. So,

under the auspices of his medical friend, Alan went
into the scheme with energy, and made such good
progress that, by 1820, he began to see clearly how,
in the course of other two or three years, he might
be able to crown his often-interrupted courtship
with the bliss of marriage. Unfortunately, among
his fellow-students at the University there were a
number of determined Radicals; and, as like draws
to like, Alan became one of the set, who fed each
other's political fires with a wonderful superfluity of
fuel. They read the most advanced authors among
poets, philosophers, divines, and politicians. They
discussed, wrote essays, and made speeches in a style
that would have astonished the most redoubtable of
their prototypes; and, occasionally, they attended
political meetings in hidden places in the city, where
things were said which ought not to have been said,
and where schemes were broached which sometimes
frightened even the student orators.

Sir John Home continued unrepentant of the
grand evil deed of his life. At this time he was devoured by hope and anxiety—by hope, because of
late Lord Carmyle had manifested symptoms of a
disease which might soon terminate fatally, and thus
afford his long and very expectant heir the ineffable
bliss of becoming a lord, and of actually possessing
as much territory as would have maintained three
German princes; and by anxiety, because Hawk was,

at the present moment, in Scotland, with his motley
retinue, named after the beasts of the earth and the
fowls of the air. There were two persons particularly
in that retinue, besides Hawk himself, whom Sir
John sincerely wished dead and buried. These were,
of course, Nightingale and Swallow. For years he
had wished them dead, but they would not die; and
Hawk, although offered irresistible bribes, declined
at last to put them finally asleep. Deeds without
names innumerable had Hawk done in his time; but
somehow this Nightingale, whom, at the instigation
of the false knight, he had for years dragged up and
down the country, had touched the only unruined
chord in his nature. In spite of himself, wrestle as
he would with his better feeling, he felt that he could
not harm the gentle, guileless creature. Sir John
had noticed this strange revulsion in the mind of
Hawk in favour of Nightingale, and it produced in
him the vague, dizzying sensations of one standing
on the edge of a precipice. With a powerful effort,
however, he crushed down these friendly premoni-
tions, and convinced himself that he would be able
to keep Hawk safe with some overwhelming bribe.
This was the stupidity of a clever man.

Hawk himself knew very well that there was great
danger in his own position; but like most men who
are powerful in some particular attribute, he sincerely
believed that the boldest emissary of justice would

think twice before assailing a person of his gigantic proportions. The healthy man seldom dreams of disease or death; and the strong man can only think that danger or defeat must come from forces physically stronger than his own. What, for instance, had Hawk to fear from such feeble, worn creatures as Nightingale and Swallow? As well might the eagle dread the dove.

Strange to say, however, while poor Swallow had for the past two years almost completely resigned herself to the iron domination of her master, the signs that Nightingale might yet permanently recover were increasing at a strange rate, and *she* had no fear of Hawk. Curious enough, too, a recent sharp illness seemed to have accelerated this change by attracting home her wandering wits—a transformation indifferently welcome to the gipsy commander, and unwelcome as poison to the cruel and avaricious knight.

One solution of his difficulty had occurred to Sir John in his growing perplexity, and it was in the proposition of it to Hawk that he resolved to offer a bribe which he thought would dazzle opposition out of existence.

'I tell you, Hawk, this will never do. She seems to have twenty lives; for any year during the long past she might have died, and still she is alive. Something must be done.'

'Had she been a man, Sir John, she would have relieved us of our sorrows long ago. But what do you propose to do?'

The pair had met by appointment, late one night at the beginning of February, in the Duke's Arms, Hamilton.

'I have a proposal to make,' Sir John answered, after a moment's reflection, 'the reasonableness of which I hope you will admit. You know, Hawk, that the boat in which we have both sailed so long is by no means a safe one.'

'Rather crank, so to speak, and growing cranker every day. I admit the truth of that; but you must not forget, Sir John, that the boat was of your building. I am simply your paid captain. It would be well, though, to have it beached somewhere out of the way.'

'My idea is that you should take the craft to some German port, and there abide with it until it goes to pieces by natural process of decay—since any more summary means is against your delicate stomach. I shall provide ample funds—name your sum. Consider it seriously, and tell me what you think.'

'That would be banishment.'

'Banishment with freedom and plenty of means, Hawk—a very different kind of thing from what we both might get in a certain eventuality.'

Sir John hung his head in saying these words. He had still some pride left, and he felt humiliated in having to utter them to a man like Hawk, in whose hands, in an evil moment, he had placed honour and life. The brigand took a great sip of brandy, pulled his beard for a minute, as if clarifying his ideas, and replied,

'I don't dislike your plan, Sir John. It fits into some of my old dreams of travel, and Germany has always had a mysterious attraction for me. But I can't leave this country for a month or six weeks.'

'Why?'

'A man like me, as you well know, has many reasons for action which cannot be spoken even to a friend. Pardon me, therefore, if I remain silent as to the aim of my journey. It is enough that I have business in the North.'

'Do you take your old route this year?'

'Not exactly. I am compelled to vary it; but in three days I join the band at Dunkeld.'

'A month is a long time,' Sir John remarked anxiously; and then he added, 'Can you trust the birds out of your sight? May they not take flight?'

Hawk smiled like one who thinks himself infallible, as he replied, 'They might take flight if I had not taken care to clip their wings. But, anyhow, there is little danger. Swallow has long been reduced to submission.'

'And Nightingale?'

'Well, she is restless, I admit, and sometimes, I fear, a little too intelligent; but she is watched by two good sentinels; so you may keep your mind easy.'

'Minds filled with the shadow of fear can never be easy.'

In saying which, Sir John Home looked like one upon whom had fallen, and was falling, the withering blight of despair. Blunted as he was by the proportion and continuation of one enormous sin, which was also a crime, he retained sufficient clearness of legal vision to be able to perceive that his victims, unless speedily disposed of, might yet arise, as from actual entombment, and blast him. Indeed, the danger seemed greater now than when the deed was newly done; for in addition to the returning mental intelligence of Nightingale, whose final disappearance from the scene Sir John so keenly desired, a suspicion still haunted the knight's mind that Hawk had lied in reference to the death of Nightingale's child. Since the incident in the hunting-field, the face of Alan Dalziel had never been absent from Sir John's mind. He now sat, silent and moody, apparently puzzled what to do, but really resolving to offer to Hawk an irresistible temptation.

'Do you see this packet, Hawk?'

'Yes; what is it?'

'It contains,' said Sir John nervously, 'ten one-hundred-pound notes.'

Hawk made an almost imperceptible movement, as if he wished to clutch so great a treasure.

'You know what I wish done in this affair. The whole thousand pounds are yours if you will consent to do the work.'

'What?'

'Leave the country at once with the two women, and never lose sight of them until they leave the earth—by whatever means.' Sir John paused significantly upon the last phrase.

'A thousand pounds appear to be a large sum,' replied the gipsy in a dubious key; 'but it amounts to this,' he added in clear incisive tones: 'you offer me a thousand pounds for the peaceful possession of the whole Carmyle estates, with the title into the bargain.'

'Hush, for heaven's sake! Did you hear a sound? Speak lower. What I offer now need not close the account between us.'

'It could not, I rather fear. Well, I accept your proposition; but only on the understanding that I don't leave the country within a month—which, indeed, I can't do. You will also let me have the money just now.'

Nothing that Sir John could urge had the slightest influence in altering the determination of Hawk.

So the cool bargain was at length agreed to; and the pair quietly left the hotel — the guilty knight somewhat comforted, and the tawny giant with feelings of contempt and triumph.

CHAPTER III.

THE ANGEL OF THE NIGHT-WATCHES.

NIGHT after night, as the angel of the still watches passed silently through the air, she paused over the city of Glasgow, and listened, as if arrested by some particular sounds.

The expression of her face slowly saddened; and at last she wept, her divine tears falling on the roofs of the troubled city.

What was it she heard, and why did she weep?

On those spring nights of the year 1820, many a little child pined and cried for bread, and had cried for months before; many a mother's heart was wrung to tears of agony because she could not appease the hunger of her children; and many a father, unable to bear the sight of his starving offspring, or the beseeching face of his wife, rushed out into the streets, where, meeting with other fathers with famishing families like himself, they took counsel together, and

became mad and reckless in the discussion of their
personal sufferings and the political wrongs of the
nation—the social sufferings, as they believed, being the logical issue of the political wrongs.

This is what the angel of the night-watches saw,
and seeing, wept.

But, farther, as she continued to gaze down upon
the moaning city, her face became troubled and dark,
like the face of the sky when a thunderstorm slowly
moves into it, thickening and broadening as it ad-
vances.

What more did the angel see?

She saw numbers of excited and wretched men
organise themselves into societies and companies.
They looked stern and determined; and they resolved to take by might what they could not get by
right. Then consultations were held, speeches made,
and resolutions adopted, which produced strange and
ominous activities throughout the city, and in all the
villages round about. In out-of-the-way corners jour-
neymen blacksmiths locked their doors, and began
to hammer at bits of iron, shape them into pike-
heads, and hide them away out of sight. Other
men scoured at old pistols, and others tinkered at
superannuated guns. Sometimes, in weavers' shops,
groups of men could be seen huddled round little
clay-built stoves, engaged in moulding bullets.

Still more did the face of the angel become dark-

ened as she turned her eye towards a particular region
of the city.

What did she see there?

She saw a large illumined chamber, wherein
were gathered a number of gentlemen, the magistrates and magnates of the city. Lord Provost Monteith presided; and an earnest discussion was going
on regarding some question about which there was
a division of opinion.

'The question is,' said his lordship, 'shall we
disperse the foolish rabble at once, or allow them to
proceed in their paths of treason until they are hope-
lessly committed, and then arrest them?'

'Let them proceed,' said a harsh decisive voice.
'Remember what a muddle you made of it two years
ago by over-haste.'

'It would, I think, be wiser, it would certainly
be more humane,' interposed the gentle voice of Lord
Carmyle, 'to stop the folly of these wretched men
now, than permit them to launch into crime. It is
a sounder policy to prevent crime than to punish
criminals.'

'By letting the evil come fully to a head, you
will be better able to crush it altogether, than by
any tinkering policy of prevention,' replied the harsh
voice.

It was decided finally to let the Radicals proceed;
whereupon, a bell being rung, a constable entered,

to whom Mr. Reddie handed a little document of instructions, whispering as he did so,

'For Captain Batwing.'

Terrible now grew the visage of the angel of the still watches, as her eye, following the official bearing the missive of the magistrates, became fixed on a solitary human figure.

What figure was it that she beheld?

She saw, in a dismal chamber in a dismal part of the city, a man sitting before a little fire, into which he was gazing earnestly, his head leaning on his left palm, and his elbow supported upon his knee. The man had once been a better man, and had seen better days. He had played a bold game for a great stake, and lost. Losing the game, he had lost hope, and with it a large portion of his self-respect. His name was blighted; and for the present he utterly despaired of self-recovery. He was roused from his bitter meditations by a cautious knock at the door; and Mr. Reddie's note was handed to him. Before opening the paper he looked at the address.

'Captain Batwing,' he read, smiling scornfully; 'an appropriate change, though too much of a conceit. But little does it matter now what name I bear: "goose" would serve the purpose; for the best name can't mend a broken man. Broken! And for what? For trying to save from ruin a set of fools! Curse them! It makes me mad to think on't!'

At this unfortunate point the man opened the paper sent by the town-clerk, and read :

'It is just as I hinted.　You are to let them proceed until their plans are completely developed—until they irrevocably commit themselves.　In taking charge of this affair, you will keep personally out of it, but work entirely by deputy.　You know the end, and have the means.　Use them boldly, and have no apprehension of the least interference.'

For a minute the man stood looking at the paper he had read, and then exclaimed excitedly :

'So be it, so be it!　Let the fools have their will, the whole measure of their folly.　We shall even help them to make and carry out their plans for political redemption.'

The man laughed like a devil.

The angel, shuddering, appealed to heaven against the wicked scheme thus so unmercifully conceived. More darkly and deeply thickened and huddled the clouds in the sky, and more hoarsely roared the blast.　But at length the edge of the vast cloud-curtain seemed lifted as by a hand ; and across the blue rift thus opened sailed the new moon, like a silver skiff issuing from the ribs of a ruined hulk ; like a soul from a dead body, but cleansed in silver fire.

The angel saw the white portent, and smiled in sad yet hopeful resignation.　Then she saw another sight in the city.

Captain Batwing was a tall straight man, of a
strenuous wiry texture; but immediately a singular
transformation became visible in his aspect.   He
bustled about his chamber, chuckling and muttering
to himself, and now and again hissing out fierce and
fiery syllables of a sneering cynical import.   At the
same time he continued to change his habiliments;
and so dexterously, that in less than five minutes he
stood in the middle of the room in the form of a
feeble old man, bent to the ground, meanly clad, and
wearing a grizzly beard.   Then he issued into the
street, and wended his way slowly and cautiously
across one of the bridges to the south side of the
river.   At the corner of one of the more hidden
streets, he paused on seeing two men apparently
scanning him keenly, and addressed them.

'Help a puir auld man!'

One of the two advanced, and asked:

'What will you have this cold night?'

'Ye're very kind, gentlemen; and if it's no owre
muckle, I'll take a wee drap brandy and a pipe.'

'All right,' answered the man; 'follow us.'

After looking about them furtively, the three proceeded deep into the shadow of a narrow *cul-de-sac*,
where a faint light glimmered from a small publichouse, into which they entered.   They were shown
into a room where a number of men were already
assembled.   The old man sat down stiffly on a seat

without speaking; and nothing was said until the landlord, having supplied refreshments, had retired, shutting the door behind him. Then the Captain took off his old coat and his grizzly beard, and stood straight up, the deformed transformed.

One of the company, who was a new ally, uttered a certain name in a tone of profound surprise.

' Hush ! Sink that name for the present, gentlemen, and henceforth know me as Captain Batwing alone. Wherever you meet me, I wish you to be particularly cautious as to how you offer recognition —rather none than run any risk. Well, you are all here ?'

' All !'

' And you are all equally willing to continue in the work ?'

' All !'

' Good. Now mark. The policy to be pursued in future is to differ from that of the past only in this, that the organisation is to be allowed to proceed as if it had the sanction of the Government, and that you are to coöperate with the societies and lend them every possible assistance. Act in all things as if you were genuine members, facilitate the development of their schemes, and report to me as usual. Our object is to let them strike the first blow —they will receive the second. Does the drilling go on as usual ?'

'More briskly than ever,' replied a man named King, who acted as Captain Batwing's first lieutenant, 'and the forging of pike-heads is also carried on with alacrity. I may mention, too, that there is to be a meeting near Paisley in a few days; and, moreover, that some important communication is expected from England with reference to the movement there.'

'Yes, I know about that; but the news from England will, I doubt, bring no consolation to them. By the way, Semple, I have something that may turn out to your advantage.'

'I should like to hear it,' answered Andrew sceptically.

'Mr. Lewis Dundas is likely to lose every penny that he has, through the failure of some great shipping speculation.'

'Serve him right; but how may that advantage me?'

'Is his daughter still living?'

'Yes, surely,' said Andrew, blushing faintly, and beginning to scent the Captain's meaning.

'In that case, if your admiration is not dead, now is your time to propose for her hand. Her father will regard you as a catch.'

'But I no longer regard his daughter as a catch. Her beauty is something, but her penny was more. Her penny gone, her beauty is nothing. I have a better plan.'

'Is it a secret?'

'Not to you. Dalziel, to whom I owe a debt, is her lover. He is also a Radical; and just let me catch him in the plot!'

'I understand,' said Captain Batwing grimly; 'but please to remember,' he added, 'that you must do nothing beyond the line of our operations. Within that line, you have ample liberty. Private wrongs cannot be allowed to interfere with the public weal, which is our great aim.'

All the company smiled a peculiar smile.

'I shall take care of that,' was Semple's sullen reply.

Captain Batwing resumed his grizzly beard and his ragged coat, and flitted silently away, the rest following, one by one.

The angel, pale with pity, veiled her face from this unhallowed den of spies. But immediately another scene, and other sounds, arrested her eye and ear.

What scene and what sounds were these?

In a small chamber, in the homely mansion of Cockmylane, sat Lewis Dundas and his cousin-housekeeper, Miss Walkingshaw. They were silent and thoughtful, and the very chamber wore a disconsolate air. At length the lady spoke.

'Then it is all gone? Is there really no hope of recovering a portion?'

'Not the slightest hope. Everything is swallowed up; but I am not without consolation.'

'Where can you possibly find it?'

'In the great fact that, if I am now penniless, I am also completely free of debt, while my creditors have received twenty shillings in the pound. Thank God for that!'

'And amen! Yet it is hard, hard, Lewis, at your age, to lose all—the labour and the savings of a lifetime.'

'In a sense it is so. But I feel, in having preserved my honour, as if I had lost nothing that was really worth having. Only one thing grieves me.'

'Ah! I guess—Christine?'

'My poor child!'

The steady heart of the philosopher was quickened, and the dry light of his eye became softened and blurred with the moist mirage of a tear. Brushing it stealthily away, he resumed,

'But I don't complain—why, indeed, should a living man complain? I have another comfort; and it will go hard, indeed, if I cannot make some provision for Christine before I die.'

'But, Lewis, you forget my savings—I place them all at your disposal. You have been a true friend to me. Allow me the privilege of remembering your goodness.'

'No, cousin; thank you, thank you! Let us

remember each other, but keep your hard-won penny-
fee. You have been of more use to Christine than
I have been to you.'

'Lewis, you are cruel!'

'Cruel, but kind. I will not risk your money,
nor any man's money, on schemes of my own.'

'But what will you do?'

'Look at my hands—and I believe, too, that I
have some brains. I shall sell my labour like other
honest men. There is no hardship in necessary
toil.'

Miss Walkingshaw could only look in the Laird's
face in tearful admiration, and murmur, 'O cousin!'
They sat in silence for some time, and then, in reply
to a question, he said,

'We must be out of this in a week; but I have
got a small house that will do well enough for Christine and myself.'

'And me?'

'My dear cousin,' said the Laird, with some
emotion, 'would it not be better for you to leave us
to our own quiet life? We could not do you any
good. I fear we could not even lodge you with proper comfort.'

'Leave you to your quiet life! You mean your
struggle with poverty—perhaps with hunger. No,
Lewis; a thousand times no! May God forgive me
for my boldness, but I will not leave you. Wher-

ever you go, I will go also. I could not live without
Christine—without you, Lewis! Pity my weakness!
Our separation would be like a divorce, we have lived
so long and so happily together. Will you not take
my money, Lewis, and use it for the good of us all ?
I want to leave it to Christine at any rate, so that
you would only be anticipating its destination by a
few years. And where could I go? I might easily
find lodgings, but never a home. I should break my
heart. Do take my money, Lewis, and let me stay.'

Miss Walkingshaw spoke in a tone of pathetic sincerity, by which she was carried away, and surprised
into revealing a secret which had long been carefully
concealed in her heart. It was only when she saw
her cousin, whom she loved and admired, thrown
almost naked upon the world, and asking no help
from anybody, not even from her, that her guard
was broken down, and she melted before his eyes.
What more could she do but weep? Lewis was
greatly affected, and said,

'My dear good cousin, you overwhelm me with
your affection and kindness. I submit to your desire—stay with us, if you can enter so poor a home.
Pardon me if for a moment I doubted whether you
would care to stay in the cloud that has come over
us. But remember, not a penny of your money will
I touch. I have faith that I shall yet do well.'

'O Lewis!' she murmured appealingly.

'Nay, Jessie, I am neither stony-hearted nor blind. I know your worth; and more than ever at this luckless moment do I feel how much of a mother and a guardian angel you have been to Christine— and to me, how much of a true wife! Calamity gives us eyes. If only I was what I have been, I would beg one favour from you, and bind you to us for ever. But I fear it would be unfair—'

'You who have never feared nor done anything unfair! Speak—let me give you that favour.'

He did not answer in words, but looked into her eyes, and touched her hand. She understood his sign, and replied eagerly, putting her hand in his,

'Take it, Lewis, and make me the happiest woman in Glasgow!'

'Jessie!'

They grasped each other's hands, and drawing fondly together, wisely and deliberately began to discuss their marriage, which they agreed to defer for a short time.

But her money? As it turned out, he was enabled to hold by his resolution not to touch a penny of it.

The angel of the still night-watches, hovering over the city, smiled a heavenly smile, and fluttered a happy wing. But as she continued to gaze, another little scene, a simple human incident, made her absolutely glow.

Miss Walkingshaw and Lewis Dundas were still discussing their new position, when the door opened, and Christine glided swiftly into the room. Going straight and noiselessly to her father, she put her arm round his neck, and tremblingly asked,

'Is it true, father, that you are ruined?'

'Why, no, my dear, I cannot say so much as that. It is true, indeed, that we have lost all our money—our worldly substance—that is all. But in losing one treasure, Christine, I have found another, which has been quite near me for years, and the value of which I knew, but did not think of possessing.'

She questioned him with her eyes, bewildered by his enigmatical words.

'Do you remember,' he continued, with signs of hesitation, 'do you mind the dream that you had about Jessie and me?'

'O! about you being married?'

'Yes. Well, that dream is likely to become a reality. In this dark hour, as some think it, when it is the custom of the world to flee from a fallen man, Jessie only clings the closer to us, and will become my wife.'

'And *my* mother,' Christine answered generously; 'O auntie, how good you are! You know my father so well, too, and I love you so much.'

'And I, Christine, love you dearly. You will be

my daughter, and we shall still be happy together. I have enough for us all.'

'But I,' said the Laird, 'will work for us all.'

'And I shall work too,' said Christine with enthusiasm.

'What will *you* work at, my dear?' asked her father, smiling.

'Don't you doubt, you dear, brave papa; I shall work miracles you can't dream of.'

'I am sure you will, my darling,' said Miss Walkingshaw, kissing Christine on the cheek; 'you will be the good angel of us both, and keep us perpetually in mind of the beauty and the goodness of heaven.'

CHAPTER IV.

A PIKE-HEAD.

'Mr. Peter Fox, Twister!' shouted the postman, at the door of a loom-shop.

'That's me,' answered Pate, from the inside of a loom, where he sat twisting a web.

'A letter.'

'Eh?—a letter for me—whaur frae?'

'Dunkeld, I think,' said the postman as he tossed the epistle to Pate.

'Dunkeld! That's the wonnerfu' toun whaur thay hanged the minister.'

'And drooned the presentor,' added Dick Flyn.

'And dang down the steeple,' superadded Andrew Hardie.

'And fuddled the bell,' concluded Willie Drappie.

Pate was puzzled at receiving a letter from Dunkeld, for he had no recollection of any friends or relations in that part of the country.

'I wonner wha it can be,' he muttered.

'It's maybe frae the Duke o' Athole,' suggested Dick Flyn, 'as ye seem to hae an increasing acquaintance wi' the aristocracy. Maybe Lord Carmyle, in visiting there, has gien the Duke an account o' his Glasgow twister frien'; and his Grace may want ye to gang north awhile, to trot ye roun' Perthshire as an example o' what a working man ought to be and believe—a twister, and yet no a Radical.'

Pate had meanwhile opened the letter, and, glancing rapidly at the end of it, he saw a name that made him start with surprise and pleasure.

'I see I'm richt,' continued Dick; 'nae sma' beer o' a correspondent could mak Pate's een lowe sae like twa cawnles. It's the letter o' a lord.'

'Weel, Dick,' remarked the twister pawkily, 'ye've aye been a guid guesser. This letter is no exactly frae the Duke o' Athole, but it's frae as guid a man, wha lives near the Duke's place; sae, ye see, ye're no sae far wrang after a'.'

'He micht weel be as guid, and yet no be sae very guid either. Is he a castle-drone or a shop-bee? That's the test.'

'That's *your* test, Dick; but it's owre ae-sided for a safe finger-post. That a' the virtues are to be seen, mair or less, in shops, I'll no deny. I've been owre muckle in shops no to ken that. But a' the virtues are, mair or less, as weel seen in castles and palaces.'

'I'm no sae sure about that,' remarked Hardie. 'If it's as easy for a camel to gang through the ee o' a needle, as for a rich man to enter the kingdom o' Heeven, that maun mean, if it means onything, that on earth rich men are nae better than they should be. Riches are no righteousness.'

'Ye're richt there, Hardie,' rejoined Pate; 'but ye maun see, at the same time, that poverty is no piety.'

'Weel, that's clear eneugh.'

'Ye're a pair o' fine philosophers,' remarked Flyn, with a touch of irony. 'How clearly ye see that ae thing is no anither! Lear levels a' invisible distinctions. And it's a grand sicht to see twa opposites shaking hauns on grun that's no debatable. There's Pate the aristocrat, for instance, and Hardie the Radical, 'greeing about a point that naebody ever disputed. It's wonnerfu'! Something's surely gaun to happen.'

'It'll no be your faut, Dick, nor the faut o' your cronies, if something doesna happen. I hope, Hardie, ye'll no be led awa in this new daft fit that's seized your Radical freens. Ye're owre guid for a tow-loop.'

'A tow-loop wad fit you,' said Willie Drappie. 'What do you ken about the Radicals?'

' 'What do I no ken, Willie? D'ye ca' that nae-thing?' And as he spoke Pate quickly snatched at something which he had seen partly sticking out of Drappie's pocket. 'What name d'ye gie that? I'm far mistaen if that's no a pike-heid. Ye've been a soger, Hardie; what do you say?'

Pate flourished the pike-head before all the men in the shop, who seemed astonished and indignant.

Dick Flyn particularly, who could have throttled Drappie, said, 'Ye're a drunken silly ass, Drappie, and wad ruin the maist heevenly cause that ever was inspired in the heart o' man.'

'Haud your tongue, Dick,' said Willie depre-catingly; 'I've as guid a richt to carry a pike as ye've to carry a pistol. And as for being a silly ass, a' that I will say is, that if ye're no a guse yoursel', it's no for want o' cacklin'. Your neb's never shut,

and ye seem as if ye were layin' some eternal egg
that never comes, and 'll no come till the Day o'
Judgment, if it comes even then.'

'This is a' nonsense,' Hardie remarked. 'I wonner, Drappie, to see ye sae foolish as carry that
bit airn on the outside o' your pouch, as if it were
some war decoration won in battle. Hae patience
far a month or twa,' he whispered in Willie's ear,
'and ye'll maybe get a chance o' makin' a pouch for
your pike in the fat o' some bloated Tory.' Then he
addressed the twister : 'I didna ken, Pate, that ye
had begun to practise the keelie trade—the pickin'
o' pouches.'

'I pity your ignorance, Hardie. But in this case,
the temptation was a'thegither irresistible. It struck
me that there was something no canny in seeing that
deidly instrument in the pouch o' a man like Drappie, whose natural weapon, as ye a' ken, is a bit
flaskie o' peat-reek frae the wimplin worm o' Glen-
killem.'

'That's the wut o' a twister,' said Flyn, 'whase
only weapon o' warfare is the stang o' a wasp or a
snuff o' caulk pouther that he flourishes atween his
finger and thoom, to mak the thrums stick thegether.
When I leuk at ye, sitting there, wi' your gray withered haffets and beady een, ye put me in mind o'
some auld warlock tying threeds o' fate.'

'D'ye ken, Dick,' answered Pate seriously, 'that

I whiles think I am a warlock. When I see some o'
you daft Radical heroes gaun about in braid daylicht wi' pikes in your pouches, as if they were tobacco-pipes; and what's mair and waur, when I hear
o' ye, and whiles see ye wi' my ain een, in the mirk
or at the deid hour o' nicht, drilling like sogers or
dizzy geese, making yoursels ready for some uncon-
scionable crime—when I see a' this, I canna help
prophesying to mysel that I'll see some o' ye in very
high places yet, the thoughtless win' making whistles
o' your exalted and craw-pickit banes.'

Young Hardie shuddered at the picture drawn
by Pate; but the rest only laughed derisively, and
bespattered the prophet with a string of powerful
epithets, in which his anti-Radical tendencies figured
in picturesque lights.

'I maun be aff to study my letter,' added Pate,
getting ready to go; 'but I say, Hardie, tak a
hint frae an auld man, and get out o' that Radical
muck.'

'Tak his advice,' said Flyn sneeringly—'become
a coward, betray your class, and maybe some o' Pate's
aristocratic freens may gie ye a bit situation to haud
their stirrups when they're gaun to ride ower the
necks o' the Radicals.'

'I've nae hope o' you, Dick,' said Pate, as he
reached the door; 'ye're ower far gane—though
Gude kens ye're nae hero. There's a squint in the

ee o' your understanding, and ye can see naething in its true licht.'

'Except a silly-daft worricow o' a lordly twister,' shouted Flyn after Pate's retreating figure .

The latter turned an instant, just as a shaggy Cossack, in galloping across the illimitable steppes, might turn and send back a parting shaft.

'Na, Dick, ye canna even see me in ony true licht. Ye're guid enough at common men and things, fish o' the mud; but it taks the soaring intellect o' the eagle to understaun' lordly character—men like me!'

Pate slammed the door of the loom-shop, and, as he stepped into the street, he wore an expression which Hogarth could have made immortal.

CHAPTER V.

THE LETTER.

WHEN Pate reached home it was dark, but, guided by long experience, he groped the way to his garret without the aid of a torch-bearer. Rummaging about, he found a bit of candle, which, after some labour, he contrived to light. There was no candlestick, either of silver or gold, or, indeed, of

any other kind of metal. But that was no hardship
to Pate Fox, who was quite satisfied with an old
bottle for a light-bearer.

'O'd, but it's cauld,' said Pate to himself, as he
stood rubbing his wrinkled hands. 'They ca' me an
aristocrat; but this is far frae being an aristocratic
abode, though, Gude be thankit, it's weel eneugh for
honest poverty. I think I may ca' mysel honest
without sprosing, and naebody could deny my poverty
wha saw me or this room—nae faut to the room
though. I've seen waur places wi' better men in
them. I may say as muckle and do nae injustice to
my ain virtues. My ain virtues! Take care, Pate,
and no be led awa' by the vanity o' human words.
Ye ken ye're no guid, and that maist virtue isna the
guidness that ony man kens he has, but the guidness
that ither folk think he has. It's a queer condition
o' things. Some men think that it's eneugh to be
thought guid, and care naething about being guid.
I doubt that'll no do up-by. My mither's way was
the best. "Peter," she used to say, "if ye hae the
riches o' grace, what signifies rags?" A very deep
question, and fu' o' truth. I'm no nae sure about
anither thing she used to say—"The rags o' the
righteous hing wi' jewels." There's maybe something
in that, but it passes me. At onyrate, it's no mony
that can wear the jewels o' adversity wi' grace. When
I see mysel through the glass o' the big shop win-

dows, I wonner I'm no sometimes taen up for a
vagabond and a thief, I'm sic a sicht. There's nae
jewels about me. "That's because ye're no righteous,
Pate." Eh! wha said that? It maun be my con-
science that speaks sae. Weel, its owre true; there's
nae righteousness, nae guid o' ony kind, in my puir,
runkled, ill-used soul. What's to come o't I dinna
ken. Wha's that?'

At this moment there was a faint tap at the
door, which Pate opened, when May Lintie stepped
timidly into the garret, to the surprise of its occupant.

' Bless me, May, ye're a sicht to see in this dark
hole o' a place. Tak a seat. There's naething wrang,
I hope? How's your faither?'

'He's nae better, Pate, and—'

'Weel, my dearie?' said the twister kindly, as
the girl hesitated.

May was pale and worn-like, and had a sad tearful expression, which touched Pate's heart.

' My mither sent me,' she said, ' to see if you
could lend her a saxpence or a shilling for twa-three
days?'

' The Lord be praised, May, I can do that. It's
no aften I hae siller; but I count it providential
that I hae some bawbees by me the now to pay back
a wee bit o' the kindness o' you and your mither to
me.'

' My kindness, Pate !'

' Ay, dearie, your kindness. Did ye no aften come and see me and sit wi' me when I was in my trouble ? Did your mither no send me mony a bite and soup, when I micht hae perished wi' hunger for onything the worl cared ? And did your faither no visit me wi' his fiddle, and cheer me up a bit, when my heart micht hae sank in the mirk o' despair ? If things like thae are no kindness, May, I dinna ken what is.'

' That was a pleasure to us, Pate, and nae trouble.'

' Weel, May, it's a pleasure to me and nae trouble to gie ye twa shillings instead o' ane ; and I hope ye'll gie me the pleasure o' doing the same again— that's to say, if ye need ony mair, for I wad rather see your faither on his feet again, and able to mak his fiddle laugh or greet like a human being, as I've often heard him do.'

' Are ye sure ye can spare that muckle, Pate ?'

' Weel eneugh, dearie, weel eneugh. Ye ken, May, that I've naebody but mysel' to maintain ; and though wark's no very thrang the now, I hae been trying to lay by in this leather bankie a bit anterin saxpence, that used to gang into the gill-stoup when Jock Makane was here.'

Pate took the two shillings from a leather purse, and put them into May's hand, as he added—

' Ye see, lass, I've twa-three left yet, sae I'm no

that ill aff. Now, if ye please, I'll see ye to your ain
close.'

'Dinna put yoursel' to sae muckle trouble, Pate.
I'm no the least fear't to gang through the streets.'

'I ken that. But the times are gay kittle,
May, and I jalouse, there's something no canny in
the win'. The Radicals are at it again wi' their
pikes and their pistols. I'll no just say they wad
meddle a bit lassie like you; but they're no saunts
ony mair than the Whigs or the Tories; and I doubt
there's a rascal or twa amang them that wadna think
twice about breaking the laws o' baith God and man.'

In escorting May homewards, Pate remembered
his letter, which the visit of the girl had put out of
his mind. He told May of it, and said that he would
come up to-morrow night and read it to them. As
they passed along the Gallowgate, Pate stopped at a
grocer's shop, and asked May to come in a minute.
The girl wondered, but the twister's object soon became clear. He ordered small quantities of tea and
sugar, which he put into May's hand, explaining that
her mother would find that to be the very best 'green
leaf' that could be got in the city, and that it was
grand for 'onybody that was no weel.' He had tried
it himself, he said, and found it first-rate for curing
'megrim pains in the heid.' But his mission was
not yet completed. When they came to a butcher's
stall, he asked for a half-pound of the tenderest

'Pope's-eye' steak that was ever kill't, with the addition of 'a wee bit suet to keep it saft and sappy' for weak teeth. This also Pate gave to May, with this reply to the girl's remonstrances,

'I believe, my doo, that this is the maist selfish thing I ever did in my life. I'm growing an auld man, and sooner or later, as ye may ken, I'll be laid on the braid o' my back. Now, ye see, when that taks place, I'll expect some guid angel, either big or wee, to come and see me in my distress, bring me a bit dainty, or maybe play the fiddle to cheer my heart. Ye ken what I mean; sae there's nae kindness ava in sending thae bits o' things to your mither. It's pure selfishness.'

'God'll reward ye, Pate!'

'Eh? Reward me for my selfishness? If He does that, May, He'll hae a gay big score to settle; for life's been wi' me just ae lang string o' self-indulgence, and that, I'm thinking, is the maist sinfu' form o' selfishness.'

'Ye're a queer man, Pate; but ye're no a guid judge o' yoursel'. Ye're aye trying to staun' in your ain licht. I ken ye better than ye think.'

'That's because ye're an angel, May, and that ither bonnie lass, wast in Anderston—'

'Miss Dundas?'

'Ay—Christine they ca' her. She's anither angel, and you twa are the only anes I ken. O'd, what een

she's got! and what a saft, sweet voice! Her words
fa' like draps o' honey on an auld dried carl like mysel'. I'm wae to think that her faither should hae
lost a' his siller. It's an awfu' douncome; but it'll
cheat me if he doesna snap his fingers at Fortune
yet, and haud his heid as high as ever.'

'That's what he's doing, Pate; and they a' seem
to be quite happy.'

'That's the kind o' thing I like to hear—it's
grand! it's grand! I've a guid mind to gang yont
and gie him my haun'.'

After seeing May safe, Pate returned to his garret
in the best of spirits, kindled a handful of fire, and
sat down to the letter, which was from Jamie Campbell.

'Jamie, my man,' said Pate, as he unfolded the
epistle, 'it's a gay surprise to me to hear that ye're
in the north and no in the south, as maist folks
thocht ye were. Let me see what ye hae to say for
yoursel'.'

Campbell's letter ran thus:

'Dear Pate,—You will nae doubt be surprised at
my lang silence. But to tell ye the truth, I had nae
heart to write; and if it wasna for something rather
queer that we've heard here, I doubt I wouldna hae
written yet.

'Before telling you this, though, let me say twa

words about oursels. Among a great many rumours
that were put in circulation about us Radicals that
gied evidence at the trial at Edinburgh, there's only
ane, Pate, that I would like to warn ye against believing. It was said that we got a lot o' money frae
the Government. I'll no speak positively for the
rest, but for mysel', I declare to you that it's as big
a lee as ever was told against an honest but misguided man. Mackinlay and me got five pounds the
piece; but it was a present frae some unknown freen,
and didna come frae the Government. The rest got
siller to pay their passage hame, and twa-three shillings mair.

'Weel, when we arrived at Falkirk on our hame-
ward journey, we took a thought into our heids that
we wadna gang back to Glasgow; and sae we turned
aff to Dunkeld, whaur the wife had some freens. We
trampit maist o' the road, and a sair journey it was,
mair especially to Willie. But he whiles got a lift
in a cart, and a bit o' the way abin Perth a big Highland drover carried him on his shouther for hale five
miles. He was as kindly a man that as ever I met.
When we got to our journey's end, we were amang
true freens; and, after a week's rest, I got wark wi'
ane o' the Duke o' Athole's foresters, and we've been
doing weel eneugh ever since. We're a' in gude
health, and nae wonner, for this, as ye may ken, is
ᵘne o' the finest and healthiest places in the country.

We live in a nice bit house, near the toun, at the side o' a grand auld wood.

'But now for the queer thing that happened the ither nicht. It was about nine o'clock, quite dark, and the wind souching eerily through the wood, when a hurried rap cam to the door. We were in the act o' preparing for bed, and I can tell ye, we got a bit fricht. After swithering twa seconds, I gaed to the door, and speered wha was there. A woman cried in great agitation, "Open and save us—quick!" There seemed to be twa o' them, and thinking they might be in danger, I opened at ance, when twa women rushed in past me to the fire, telling me for the love o' God to bar the door. That I did in double-quick time, as ye may guess. But the funniest part o' the thing was that when they were in I couldna get them out, nor could I weel understand the story they tried to tell. If you had heard it, you would hae thought at first it was a' about hawks, eagles, lions, tigers, cats, deer, swallows, nightingales, owls, and ither animals. The real truth seems to be that they belanged to a camp o' wanderin' tinklers that hae been stravaigin' about this part o' the country for some time, and wha, instead o' human names, gang by the names o' birds and beasts. It's my opinion that the twa women hae been kept in the camp against their will, and that some foul wrang or crime has been done against them. Their great terror appears to be

a man named Hawk. They implored us to gie them
lodgin' until they could find means to gang to Glasgow or Hamilton. What could we do? Mary took
pity on them, and she resolved to shelter them until
a' danger o' pursuit might be past. But I doubt
they'll no be able to escape.

'It's quite clear to me that the puir creatures hae
suffered a great deal. One o' them especially appears
as if she had been quite crazy; but I'm far mista'en
if she hasna seen better days. There's something
about her that's no quite commonlike, and her manner o' speaking is better than the style o' the tinklers. Her name is Nightingale, and she's no unlike
a nightingale in the gentleness o' her nature and
the saftness and sweetness o' her voice. Swallow
is the name o' her companion, though some might
think that they baith cam out o' the ae nest, they
are sae kindly and freenly, only Swallow seems to
look on Nightingale as her superior; and that's my
ain belief.

'You'll maybe think this a gay queer story, Pate;
but what I'm gaun to say will make it appear mair
sae. The twa are often in deep conversation, and
for the maist part, they speak sae low that it's no
easy to hear what they say; but whiles they are no
sae guarded, especially at nicht when they gang ben
the room to the bed that we hae made up for them.
Now, Pate, what I'm gaun to say is as true as death.

Baith Mary and mysel' hae heard them mair than
ance speak o' Sir James Douglas, Lord Carmyle, Sir
John Home, and a baby; and every time we hear
thae names mentioned, Nightingale seems to moan
and greet in the maist distressing manner. What it
a' means is clean past our power to guess. It's just
possible that there's some nonsense in't; but Mary
thinks quite differently, and she has a notion that
ane or baith o' the women hae been sair wranged.
Was there no some queer story about Lord Carmyle
when he was Sir James, in the auld lord's time?
Mind, Pate, I dinna mean ony ill in asking the question; and to tell you the truth, I wouldna hae written
about this ava, if it hadna been for Mary, wha thinks
that somebody else besides oursels should be made
acquaint wi' the story.

'The women are here yet. They keep weel in
the house, and never gang out through the day; but
they mean to be aff as soon as the weather grows a
wee milder. It was a gude thing for us that they
had some siller, or we couldna hae keepit them sae
lang. I hae gien them a hint or twa about the safest
way to gang south, and if they dinna change their
plans, or be catched by their enemy Hawk, they will
be in Glasgow about the beginning o' April. It'll be
a weary journey for them, as they maun fit it a' the
way.

'Fareweel, Pate. We send you our truest love,

inspired by mony thoughts, baith sad and happy, o
auld lang syne.

'Is it true what I hear, that the Radicals are at
their auld tricks again? I think it's a great pity.
At least, my experience o' the past is a'thegither
against a policy o' physical force. I'm no a bit the
less convinced than I was, that there's something
rotten in our system o' government, and that it
ought to be speedily mended; but everything maun
be done by peaceful means. The battles maun be
fought between the opposing forces o' ideas armed
wi' the weapons o' human wisdom and eloquence.
That was Richmond's view. Speaking o' Richmond,
d'ye ken onything about him? He was a strange
man that. I heard that he was in Edinburgh at the
time o' our trial, gaun about like a tortured ghost,
because the part he took in the business was exposed,
and himsel' branded as a black-hearted spy. I dinna
think he was sae bad, although you were convinced
he was a' that, and mair. But nae man can be fairly
judged by looking only at ae bit o' his life. If onybody were to judge *me* by the part I took in what
you used not untruly to ca' the Gallows Club, they
would put me down for a rank idiwut, which wouldna
be true, as ye ken weel eneugh. I think, Pate, I
maun hae been wrang in the heid then, wi' the hunger
and the dark prospect o' the times. I hear things
are gayan bad again in Glasgow amang the weavers.

God pity them and help them! That's my warst wish.

'A word about Willie. He's at the schule every day, but he works wi' me in the woods for twa hours in the afternoons. He aften speaks o' Glasgow; and in particular, he minds yoursel', May Lintie, and Christine Dundas, wha seems to hae the power o' enchanting everybody. If Willie wasna only a bit callant, I would say he was in love wi' Christine. He makes his mither and me whiles laugh in our sleeve wi' his warm talk about her. Is there ony chance o' Dalziel and her gaun thegither?

'For the last time, I maun say fareweel. I would like to see ye, Pate; but I'm thinking that canna be for a while yet. If you see the Dundas family, gie them our sincere love. We can never forget them, nor what they did for us in the dark and miserable days o' the past.

'Now, Pate, hoping that you are weel, and that you will be able to write me a bit note,

'I subscribe mysel' your affectionate

'Auld Freen,

'JAMES CAMPBELL.

'P.S.—Mary has compelled me to add, that you might do waur than tell Lord Carmyle about the story o' the twa women. She doesna believe that his lordship can be onyway to blame; and he may be able to find out if ony injustice has been done. Mary thinks, too, that you might keep a look-out for the twa travellers in April. I'm compelled to write this, Pate; but it seems to me that baith suggestions are quite unreasonable.—J. C.'

'Hech!' said Pate, after finishing Campbell's letter; 'this is a bonnie story. Twa women! That's a gay haunfu', Jamie; and what I'm to do wi' them, if they should come this way, is a tickler o' a question. I wadna wonner a bit if they hae been wranged. It seems to me that women are aye wranged. But about telling Lord Carmyle, that's a doubtfu' point. What he can hae to do wi' them is no very clear; though I believe there was some queer story about him in his young days. But it's eneugh to be a lord to hae a hale volume o' big lees tell't about ye. It's the nature o' riches and high position to breed ill rumours. And Sir John Home, too. Weel, if a' stories be true, he's nae better than he should be— an airn-faced, soople-souled lawyer, wi' the jaw o' a prize-fechter, and an ee like a coal-pit. What's waur, he's Lord Carmyle's heir. I wadna like to hae a man like him for my heir—that's to say, if I had onything to leave. Twal o'clock,' muttered Pate, as he heard midnight clanged from a neighbouring steeple. 'I canna settle the nicht what I'll do the morn. As the lawyers say, I maun tak the case to avizandum, and mysel' to bed.'

Which Pate did, after supping on one half scone, and a smoke.

CHAPTER VI.

LOVE AND POLITICS.

WHILE Pate Fox is considering Jamie Campbell's letter in that mysterious region or condition called ' avizandum,' which is supposed to be favourable to the production of wise and just conceptions regarding whatever is taken thither, the current of our story drags us into a very different atmosphere.

For one moment, however, let us linger in a quiet bay at the edge of the rushing stream.

Alan Dalziel had come from his lodgings in College-street to visit Christine Dundas in the new home which her father had provided for them. This place was on a much humbler scale than Cockmylane, and afforded just comfortable space for three—Mr. Dundas, his daughter, and Miss Walkingshaw.

The tide in the affairs of Lewis had already begun to turn. When it became known that misfortune had befallen him, his services were at once sought by the largest ironfounder in the city, who gave him the charge of all his works. This engagement exactly suited his peculiar genius; so that, with no effort of his own, but solely on account of his ability, and the honourable character of his failure, he was once more made comparatively comfortable, if not independent.

Alan had been greatly shocked at the ruin of his friend, his feeling being naturally intensified by his relation to Christine. She was now dearer to him than ever. The misfortune of her father only drew him more closely to her. It must be said, however, that in Alan's grief there was a sort of satisfaction, arising from the fact that Christine was not so far above him in fortune as she used to be, which had the effect of making him feel less uneasy and more hopeful.

Yet his courtship did not seem to prosper exactly to his liking. His love for Christine could only increase; but her liking for him, while not decreasing, was not apparently making any special progress. He did not see that her love was perfect, and could not become more imposing and enchanting to his hungry imagination. He was unable to comprehend that any existing imperfection lay in himself, or in the potent circumstance that, while love on both sides was ripe, he was not in a condition to pluck its perfect fruit. Christine could do nothing but wait and nurse her tender passion; and what the position imperatively demanded of him was to make strenuous endeavours to achieve a position in which he could fairly seek to crown the hope with the fact of marriage.

Both Christine and her father knew that Alan

was making good progress with his medical studies. Dr. Bannatyne had told them as much. But they knew also that, along with other students, Alan was again attending political meetings; and that, therefore, considering the exceedingly practical aims of the Radicals, there was some danger of his once more ruining his prospects. Alan seemed, in fact, to be devoured by a species of political infatuation. He only laughed at the cautions and counsels of Lewis and Dr. Bannatyne.

'If you allow us liberty to think,' he said on one occasion, 'you must permit us also to act according to the wisdom of our thinking.'

'But not according to the folly of it,' Lewis promptly replied.

'Who, then, is to distinguish between folly and wisdom in thinking?'

'Certainly not the fool. Somebody with a modicum of brains must do that—somebody who will not, with open eyes, thrust his hand into a blazing fire, and expect to take it out unscorched. Fearless you may think; but you cannot think without sowing the seeds of regret; and your free actions are dogged by hound-like penalties.'

'Is that philosophy?' asked Alan.

'It is sad truth.'

'Then it comes to this—that we had better do nothing, lest we do something wrong.'

'That's the natural remark of those who have two courses before them, and who, having an overwhelming desire to select the one which is most striking, but least wise, take refuge in total inaction if checked in their folly.'

'You are cutting the wings of adventure,' replied Alan.

'If adventure takes the wings of a goose—yes.'

'Yet a goose may lay a golden egg.'

'It's the function of a goose to lay eggs; and a very good function it is. But what, Alan, would you say of the goose which, instead of being content to lay its egg day after day, deliberately rips itself up, in the hope of clutching in a moment the product of years ?'

'It would be a goose indeed.'

'Yet that is precisely what the Radical fowl is again threatening to do. Over all the city, and in other places, a low ominous cackling is heard. People are growing pale in the face, and are beginning to tremble. But let me tell you that the goose will only rip herself against the steely claws and relentless beak of the eagle; and instead of getting all the golden eggs of freedom at once, as she expects, she will only, I fear, find agony and death. In plain language, Alan, the Government will have no mercy this time. I have reason to know as much; so take warning. Moreover,' added Lewis significantly,

'young men with their fortunes to make ought not
to slap Fortune on the face.'

'He means me,' thought Alan, retiring from the
wordy contest. 'Yet how often have I heard him
say that success in any great cause is only possible
through a series of great sacrifices !'

This conversation had taken place some days before Alan's present visit to Christine; and he was
surprised to find that her sentiments closely re-
sembled those of her father. In reality, nothing
could be more natural; yet nothing could be more
disagreeable to him. He had, so to speak, been
politically nursed in Cockmylane; and it seemed to
him that all he had learned there pointed logically
to action, under certain national conditions. From
personal observation, and from listening to the ha-
rangues of a select few of his fellow-students and
some of the popular Radicals in the city, Alan felt,
with many others, that the season of speculation was
past, and that the time for action had come. According to the popular orators, the country was going to
wreck, trade was ruined, the people were starving;
yet the Government were making no effort to prevent
total destruction. On the contrary, they were taking
things coolly and complacently, and rather enjoying
the clamours for reform as an interesting kind of
hallucination on the part of a few impertinent theor-
ists. As for the misery said to be abounding in the

country, they didn't believe it. They considered that
the country was pretty comfortable, and that the
people would never have dreamed of being miserable
if they had not been informed of the fact by a flying
squadron of brigand-demagogues, who scoured the
country scattering falsehood and fire in places, and
among peasantry and workmen, hitherto innocent of
all political doubt and discontent.

These were the views entertained among the Radicals regarding the attitude of the Government towards the country and the Reform movement.

The lovers had met. Alan was hopeful and im-
petuous; Christine calm and intense. They had been
studying each other for some time, as lovers will do
who have passion in their hearts and speculation in
their eyes. Although still demonstrative in his affection, Alan was insensibly growing more guarded and
refined in the expression of it. There was less panto-
mime, though not less feeling, in his manner than
there used to be in the earlier stages of their courtship. This was partly due to the widening and deepening influence of his own experience acting upon
his naturally noble nature. His contact with the
University, too, was producing intellectual effects of
the most promising kind; though, in the mean time.
these effects were rendered somewhat chaotic by the
almost revolutionary freedom of the student life in
which he mingled. But one of the sources of Alan's

growing refinement, and by far the subtlest, was the
influence of Christine herself, whose utter purity,
sweetness, openness, and truthfulness of nature never
failed to affect the strongest character with whom
she came in contact. Her own father confessed her
healing and purifying influence. Her beauty was,
no doubt, a potent element in the silent power she
wielded; for nobody with a soul could look into that
face and those eyes, so luminous with the light of
innocence and intellect, and not feel that he was in
the presence of a superior being.

Alan was more than ever enthralled with Christine, but he began to perceive and feel something of
the awe which perfect beauty and perfect goodness
in woman always inspire in the minds of honourable men; and therefore, as we have said, he was
becoming more reticent and delicate in the expression and demonstration of his passion. The freedom
of the Scotch boy-lover had nearly vanished; but
there was coming in its stead something of the calm,
the tender considerateness, which distinguishes the
deepening intelligence of the true worshipper.

The conversation of the lovers had murmured
through the usual windings of sweetness, hope, and
fear. There were recurring silences, which were,
however, only silences of the tongue. Their eyes
continued to speak more eloquently than their lips,
except when these were blown together by the

sweeter gusts of passion. But even in such colli-
sions, though always legitimate in lovers, Alan sel-
domer indulged, though not from any lack of desire.

'Yes, Christine,' said Alan, 'I like it more and
more. It seems to me that the profession of the
physician is far nobler than that of the lawyer. It
is wholly good. Every success of the healer is a
benefit. It involves the destruction or mitigation of
pain or disease. Every success of the lawyer leaves
a sting behind it in the heart of the defeated client.'

'You are right, I think, as to the physician, in
whose art there is something divine, and whose work
is like that of the Divine Physician, who went about
doing good. I am glad you like the profession.
There can be no fear of failure?'

As she put the question, she looked anxiously
into his eyes.

'No; I think not. And in two years, Christine
—how long that period seems!—if all things go
well, I shall be able, I hope, to speak definitely of
some such settlement as may please your father, and
safely warrant our union.'

'In two years—if all things go well?' she repeated, faintly interrogative. 'Less than two years
ago, who would have thought of an occurrence like
that which has happened to my father?'

'Who, indeed!' he answered; 'and little more
than two years ago, who would have dreamed in the

wildest delirium of the revelation which made me in a moment both fatherless and motherless ?—made me nobody ?'

' Don't, Alan ! To us, you are not less than you were—to me, you are more.'

' That's your goodness—your nobleness, Christine,' Alan replied, his eyes sparkling as if he had heard her statement for the first time. ' The knowledge that I am somebody to you—that I have still your love—repays me a thousand times for all the pangs I may have suffered. If my love could equal such love—'

' And does it not, Alan ? Remember,' she said, smiling, ' I am now a penniless lass, with not even a brief pedigree, and therefore no match for a gentleman. I have heard that a doctor may pick and choose among the best families, yet the change of fortune which has come over us has not frightened you away. Is there no merit in that ?'

' If there is any merit in loving where one cannot choose but love—in not being false where there is every temptation to be true—then there may be some merit in my not playing the fool and the traitor ! Your love is worth a world of fortunes !'

Their eyes met in answering flashes.

But the report of a pistol or gun in the neighbourhood at once set them on a new track of talk, which contrasted unfortunately with the previous strain of tenderness. It suggested the Radicals, at whose bold manœuvres the city was again getting into a condition of scare. This was the one cruel rock which was always threatening to wreck the peace of the lovers; and to-night they were all but splitting upon it in spite of the most skilful pilotage. As it was, Alan went away in a very uncomfortable mood; while Christine was left in a condition of miserable apprehension.

There is nothing like a snuff of politics or a puff of theology for smoking Love out of Paradise, or letting the Devil in.

It was as if Christine had said, ' There is a lion in the way, Alan dear. Beware lest he tear you to pieces.'

And it was as if Alan had replied, ' You are mistaken, dearest; it is not a lion, but a very harmless, decent, and useful beast of burden. It is only the poor man's ass, who is crying for a bite of hay from the national haystack. He is quite a harmless creature, and will injure nobody, if nobody injures him. At all events, he won't injure me.'

But Alan's assurances could not allay Christine's fears; and so their conversation, which had begun so sweetly, and had gone on for some time so wisely, ended in mutual distress. The lady tried all she could to believe in the wisdom of her lover; but knowing how accessible he was to political influ-

ences, and particularly to those influences issuing
from the most daring section of the Reformers, she
seemed to feel that his understanding would be no
match for his imagination.

Had she been able to follow the footsteps of Alan
that night after he left her, she would have received
proof of the prophetic character of her feelings.

CHAPTER VII.

A RADICAL STAMPEDE.

THE College examinations were to come off in
April, and Alan had begun to prepare for the contest. Dr. Bannatyne, whose medical *protégé* Alan
was, had predicted to Christine that her lover would
come off with flying colours. Alan entertained confident hopes of the same kind. Yet to-night, instead
of going straight to his lodgings to continue his preparations for the anatomical, physiological, and medical combat, he allowed himself to be drawn in a very
different direction.

On leaving Christine, with feelings approaching
to bitterness, he drifted aimlessly through a variety
of streets, until, on reaching the Cross, he was over-
hauled by a person who addressed him quietly, thus:

'I'm glad to see ye, Mr. Dalziel.'

Alan looked hard at the speaker for a moment, for it was dark, and at length said,

'Hardie ?'

'Ay; are ye gaun to the meeting ?'

'Which meeting ?'

'Brigton. Your freen' Macpherson, and twa or three o' the Provisional, are to be there. Important news hae been received frae England.'

'What of the meeting that was to be held in the Drygate ?'

'It's the same. But some suspicious character has been seen spying about the place for the last twa days, and it was thought better to meet in the East.'

They walked slowly along the Gallowgate, conversing quietly as they went. Alan told Hardie that he had to visit a friend who was unwell, and he was not sure whether he would be in time for the meeting. It is just probable that he would have preferred visiting Bob Lintie, whom he regarded as a sort of patient of his own; but before reaching the entry to Bob's house, they were overtaken by Macpherson, who was one of Alan's fellow-students, accompanied by another celebrated orator of the Radical Clubs. The influence of these two was irresistible, and he went with them, though not without a pang, as the face of Christine rose in his imagination, full of warning and anxiety.

When they reached the supposed place of meeting in Bridgeton they were informed by a person who seemed to be there for the purpose, that as a farther precaution the friends were to assemble on the banks of the Clyde immediately north of Rutherglen. The man could not give them any special reason for this change of place, though Hardie was no way surprised.

After some hesitation on Alan's part, all four proceeded to the place of rendezvous, walking, however, in twos, a little separated, so as not to attract notice. At the east end of the Main-street, the two parties joined, went along the bridge to the south side of the river, and then walked up the bank. On approaching the meeting-place, a man, planted as a sentinel, stood out from behind a large tree, and blew a whistle, which was answered by another whistle farther up the river. Hardie on this put his finger to his mouth and whistled also, as if in jest.

'All right,' said the man, who whistled again, the meaning of his signal being that only friends were approaching.

The scene, so far as it was visible in the blinking starlight and the clouded moonlight, was interesting and significant. Standing on the high bank of the river, and looking south, Alan saw in the field beneath a crowd which he felt sure could contain no fewer than two hundred persons. This was an exaggeration produced by the nature of the night, which, with the aid of a few human beings, multiplied others, of airy and fantastic shape, out of their own shadows. The real persons there were, with two exceptions, Radicals. One of these exceptions, who was restlessly hovering about, approached the new arrivals as near as possible without being detected, and peered into their faces. This was the act of a moment, for as soon as he saw Alan Dalziel he shrank back as if he had been stung, and, like the witches in *Macbeth*, made himself air, into which he vanished, though not quite from the locality.

At the sound of a low cautious whistle, the Radicals gathered in a close group, in the centre of which stood the conductors of the meeting. The proceedings do not call for any detailed description, particularly as they were in their salient features very much like those of other meetings which we have somewhat minutely recorded in the earlier chapters of our story. There were several energetic speeches. The lamentable state of the country was, as usual, painted in powerful colours; the wickedness of the Government was exposed and denounced; and the Radicals were called upon to arise in their might, and fearlessly assert their rights, relying for success upon their strong right arms and the righteousness of their cause. What the Government ought to do, but would not do, for the salvation of the country, they ought to be compelled to do. That was the keynote of the oratory, the fierce rhetorical character of which was well calculated to set the imagination of the listeners on fire with enthusiasm. There was a remarkable unanimity of feeling, which may perhaps be partly accounted for by the solemnity of the scene. Under such a wide, calm, wandering roof of cloud and star, and dull moony splendour, opposition seemed unnatural and impossible.

When the audience had listened to the speeches, and were in a state of molten credulity, it was announced by a new orator that England was ready to rise. This, he asserted, was no idle statement, but a fact which a few days would verify, when the Scottish Reformers would hear of something which would astonish them. The speaker strongly urged that a meeting of delegates, from the principal centres of Reform in Scotland, should at once be called together in some safe and convenient place, to consider the best means of responding to the event which was about to happen over the Border.

The meeting believed the speaker. There was in the idea of something being about to happen precisely that element of mystery which lifts the political plotter as by the hair of the head into a romantic region of hope—a region all the more attractive that it is overshadowed by fear or guarded by terror.

After some farther earnest consultation, a signal was given, and the whole assembly formed themselves into order on the level field, when they were put through a course of military exercise by a person who must have been a soldier. Alan and Hardie were the only persons who did not join in the operations — the former standing apart watching, and the latter attending the drill-sergeant, apparently assisting him with advice. Hardie had served in the Militia.

The drill had continued for nearly half an hour when suddenly another loud whistle was heard from one of the sentinels. In an instant the whole corps stopped, and stood in silent and anxious expectation. A double whistle was then heard from the same sentinel. As this meant danger, there was an immediate preparation to stand on the defensive, or do something else.

In about a minute the Radicals were startled by a strange sight. They saw moving up the bank of the river some half-dozen lights; and as nobody could be seen bearing them, they looked as if they were carried by invisible spirits, or were dancing through the air, self-supported. The boldest Radical there held his breath for a considerable time, and all of them readily obeyed the word of command to lie flat on the ground, although the grass was uncomfortably wet. Alan declined to lie down, and

preferred the shelter of a tree, into the fork of which
he vaulted with ease. The lights continued to advance, and to Alan, who had a better view of them
from his perch, they seemed to be carried each by
a shadowy figure, whose face looked thinner and
paler than any moonbeam. On reaching nearly opposite the horizontal Radicals, the strange torch-
bearers stopped suddenly and formed themselves
into a group, and Alan saw the six pale faces go
together as if in consultation. It was a strange
mysterious sight, and sent a shudder through the
heroic spirits lying on the ground.

'Whew!' said Alan, suddenly and quietly; 'I
see!—I understand!'

But nobody but himself saw or understood the
fiery phenomena in the precise light in which he did,
and everybody remained silently sealed to the field.
At length, the consultation of the lights seemed to
result in some resolution, for they immediately
began to advance down the bank towards the Radicals, making at the same time a strange clinking
noise, like that which soldiers make when getting
ready to fire a volley. This demonstration produced
universal palpitation amongst the rank and file of
the patriots. Even the leaders were completely mys-
tified. So that when the moving lights, adding voices
to themselves, exploded in a terrific shout and rushed
forward, making also metallic noises, the Radicals

could bear it no longer, but rose and fled in the wildest state of excitement, Hardie, the drill-sergeant, and Macpherson, one degree less daunted than the rest, hanging in the rear.

Alan still retained his position in the tree, both amazed and amused at the sudden stampede. After a few minutes, as he saw the lights returning along the field, he dropt to the ground and walked towards the bridge, saying to himself:

'Who would have thought that six colliers, going to their work, with lamps on their heads, spoons rattling on their pannikins, and with a shout and a rush could have put to flight scores of Radicals. The Rights of Man will hardly be won by these men, I fear.'

But Alan was not the only person who was not frightened from the field; and, as he went along at a leisurely pace, the same person who had shrunk from his eye now came slinking after him in the dark, crawling rather than walking.

What did the man want?

As Alan was about to descend to a lower level, towards the river's edge, a pistol-shot broke the stillness of the night, and a bullet whistled past within a foot of his ear. Reaching the friendly shelter of a sycamore, Alan paused to reflect.

'Could that bullet be meant for me?' he thought; 'and who could be so rash and base? It is not pos-

sible, surely, that Semple would seek revenge in that
way! I cannot think it.'

It was true, nevertheless, for no other hand was
guilty of the crime.

Possibly Andrew Semple did not mean to commit
murder, but only to scare Alan, whom he regarded
as his enemy. Yet when he had fired, and watched
a moment to see the result, he seemed dissatisfied,
and growled:

'A wasted bullet, by Jove!' Then after a little
he added, 'It is perhaps better. I may find a safer
way to wing the bastard.'

This attempt to murder Alan's character with a
weak pun, after missing his body with a bit of lead,
was characteristic of Semple, who had only a butch-
erly sense of humour.

Before retiring to his innocent pillow that night,
Andrew spent a half-hour with Captain Batwing, to
whom he communicated several bits of information
regarding the military movements of the Radicals in
the various districts of the city; but he concealed
the fact that he had himself been having a bit of
pistol practice at the brain of Alan Dalziel.

CHAPTER VIII.

CAPTAIN BATWING.

EVENTS had thickened lately; and feeling was still quickening in all centres of political activity. The Radical pulse was beating fearfully under a bare aspect and threadbare sleeve. Hunger stalked through the city with a shadow at its side, whispering in its ear suggestions of fearful import. Those suggestions fructified and blossomed more and more in treasonable speeches; and these, in their turn, were more and more threatening to burst in deeds of fire and blood. Pike-forging, bullet-moulding, and scouring of old guns still continued; and in various hidden places round the city the stillness of midnight was broken by the tramp, tramp of Radical companies, drilling and preparing for the day which was to doom a tyrannical oligarchy to destruction, and to see inaugurated the reign of real representative government, which meant universal suffrage, annual parliaments, equality and fraternity, peace and plenty.

Inspired by the stirring news from England, a great effort was made by the select committee; and on the 22d February a general congress of delegates from all the Radical unions in the west of Scotland had been held in a field at Meikleriggs, near Paisley. Its success was equal to the secrecy and the skill with which it was planned. Two or three great orators were there; and the mighty speeches they delivered thrilled the welkin and all the souls under it in that particular field. The meeting was held at night, which made the proceedings more solemn and impressive. The delegates had selected a spot where a number of dark Scotch pines afforded some sort of shelter and defence against the observation of any undesirable eye that might be spying about.

There, in that grove, like a company of political Druids, they discussed their plans, which, if boldly and faithfully carried out in conjunction with the plans of their English brethren, seemed incapable of failure. The leading speaker, in an oration of singular pathos and power, invoked the spirit of the national patriot, Sir William Wallace, imploring that he might be with them to inspire and aid them in their holy and patriotic enterprise. Finally, grasping hands, they swore fidelity to each other; and after appointing and dispatching a delegate to the north of England, they separated, and returned home in a mixed mood of heroism and anxious expectancy.

A few days brought intelligence of the great feat which was to be done in England, and which was to act as the signal for the Scottish risings. But the intelligence fell upon the Caledonians like a thunderbolt. The great English attempt had failed; or, rather, the English patriots, having been betrayed, were arrested before they had delivered the great blow which was to shake tyranny to pieces and begin the regeneration of the country. The programme of the conspirators, of whom Thistlewood was the leader, was perfect of its kind—a genuine work of art. It proposed to assassinate the Ministry; that Ministry which had hung about the neck of the country for years, and was strangling it to death; that Ministry which had waved back the Reformers with a haughty hand—had, so to speak, stamped on the petitions of the people, and superciliously closed their ears to the despairing cries of distress which went up from all the cities in the land.

Thistlewood was betrayed, and he and four companions were arrested, imprisoned, tried, and found guilty; and on the 1st of May following they paid with their lives the penalties of their blind patriotism and criminal daring.

The failure of the English initiative by the arrest of the leaders produced a confounding effect on the Scotch Radicals. They knew not what to do; and for a time there was some probability that the societies would fall asunder. Many of the leaders actually withdrew; but their places were instantly filled by others of equal spirit; so that by the end of March the organisation was more complete than ever. All the surrounding districts were put in close communication with Glasgow, as the vital centre of Radical authority; a plan of insurrection was arranged; and all that seemed necessary was to name the hour for setting the fire to the torch.

At this critical juncture, Captain Batwing appeared to be particularly busy. He looked like a man in the expectation of great events. He flitted about the city, generally under the cloud of night, in a restless, yet decisive, manner, like one who knows his business thoroughly well, and is certain of performing it triumphantly.

Several of his night rambles took him to those secret corners in fields and by-lanes where companies of Radicals happened to be drilling. Other of his visits were to small smiths' ships, where a quiet stroke of business was done in the forging of pike-heads. But the Captain seemed more intent simply in observing how the secret plans of the campaign were ripening than in aiding the movement by personal suggestion. Any assistance which he lent to the leaders of the conspiracy did not issue from himself directly, but from a half-dozen lieutenants of whom he had command. These gentlemen were members of the various Radical unions in the city. They were shrewd and intelligent men, but wholly indifferent to the moral aspect of the work in which they had deliberately engaged. Being Radicals in appearance, they assisted the movement with energy, and were always on the side of the most

sweeping and uncompromising measures. Being
spies in reality, they reported nightly to Captain
Batwing every point of the Radical scheme as it
gradually assumed a decisive form. In his turn, the
Captain unfolded the scheme to Mr. Reddie; so that
the authorities, being fully cognisant of all that was
going on, were able to make such preparations as
would enable them to shape the issue in their own
favour, and most fatally to the conspirators.

Yet Captain Batwing, as commander-in-chief of
the spies—or, to put it less offensively, as chief of
the unofficial detectives—was not a happy man. He
knew that the conspiracy would be shivered to pieces
on the bristling lines of authority; but any one looking at his face, and watching his manner, might have
been justified in thinking that it was he who was
doomed to destruction.

One evening near the end of March, he sat in his
room in the city. He was reading Godwin's *Political
Justice;* and now and again he would make a pause,
and appear to brood deeply over the passage he had
just finished. On the whole, however, there seemed
little satisfaction in the study. His readings grew
shorter and his ruminations longer. At length he
dashed the book on the floor, saying as he did so:

'It is wonderful how that book has changed.
When I read it first it seemed little less than divine;
and now—faugh! Drivel! mere drivel!'

Then, after a turn or two through the room in tragic style, he smiled bitterly, and spoke :

'Well, it may be myself that has changed. Books are always of the same opinion to the fixed mind. But the ideas in books change their appearance with the changing world, for better or for worse. Is it better with me, or is it worse ?'

He did not answer his own question, except by a doubtful shrug of his shoulders ; and perhaps the restless gleam of his eye was full of negative meaning. For the third time he looked at his watch, and said,

'They are late.'

But the persons to whom he referred were only a few minutes later ; and immediately they entered he assaulted them with swift interrogatives.

'Well, King, what progress in the east ?'

'All seems ready, Captain.'

'In Glasgow, no doubt ; but what of Cambuslang, Hamilton, Strathaven ?'

'In all these towns there are numbers hot for action ; but the feeling is most decidedly warlike in Strathaven.'

'That's owing to the influence of James Wilson, who is a Reformer of the boldest type.'

'I'm not so sure about that,' replied King. 'From what I was able to observe, Wilson seems rather to be led than to lead in this affair. That may be only

cunning on his part, for he appears to be as keen a
Radical as MacIntyre or any of the rest.'

‘If Wilson were less a sensible man than I know
him to be,’ replied the Captain, ‘I should call him
a fool for his present conduct; if he were less up-
right, I should set him down as a sly old fox. What
news from the west, Lees?’

‘In Paisley, as usual, all is fire and fury. Pinky
and Spiers, the inspiring spirits of the town, have
been in a continual blaze for the past week. They
have one great scheme in their eye.’

‘What is it?’

‘To besiege and take Dumbarton Castle.’

This announcement produced a unanimous burst
of laughter; and the Captain said,

‘Like Pinky, like Paisley, and like Spiers. They
aim high—they will probably sack a loomshop. We
must none the less, however, give the hint to have
the Castle garrisoned and provisioned. What say
you? These cobwebs show how the wind blows.
Anything from the north?’

‘So far as the city is concerned,’ replied Turner,
the man thus addressed, ‘the spirit of the movement
is at white heat. In the towns north and east of the
city, there is plenty of talk, as usual; but I doubt
whether many will join the contemplated rising when
it comes to the point.’

‘Little dogs,’ the Captain remarked, ‘that haven’t

the courage to beard a rat often bark loudest. Well, Craig, how do matters look in the south—particularly in that remarkable town where wisdom was first born, and where it will last die?'

'Pollokshaws?'

The Captain tossed an affirmative with his head.

'The folk o' the Shaws, Captain, hae a reputation for being able to play twa tunes at the same time on every string o' their fiddle.'

Captain Batwing glanced keenly at Craig; but as the latter seemed unconscious of any blunder, the Captain, who belonged to Pollokshaws, only answered in a thick whisper, 'Ay, ay.'

'At the same time,' continued Craig, 'although it's no easy just to say what they'll do, still, if we may judge by outward signs, there'll be some noise in the town, and maybe ayont it, if the Radicals really should set licht to the poother.'

'Now,' said the Captain, after brief reflection, 'have you been able to discover anything farther as to whether a definite plan of operations has been discussed?'

To this query, which was addressed generally, Andrew Semple replied with an air of importance,

'I told you before, Captain, that I had heard hints regarding a preliminary proclamation—'

'Well!'

'Well, it is all settled; and not only so, but I have contrived to hook a copy of it.'

'In the quarter to which I directed you?' asked the Captain, whose eyes absolutely exploded in light as he took and glanced over the document. 'This is really a vital link in the conspiracy, gentlemen, and shows that our work is drawing to a close. Thank you, Andrew; you have in you the making of a great diplomatist. Is there any other fact?'

'There is one,' said King, 'or rather what looks like one, although it may turn out to be the dream of a driveller.'

'In affairs like this,' the Captain remarked, 'we can't afford to despise even dreams. Everything is true until it is proved to be false. What is it?'

'It refers to a plan of action. It begins with a proposition to march quietly and suddenly on Carron Iron Works, seize the cannon there, and then—'

'Well, and then?'

'The next step,' said King, smiling, 'is to besiege Stirling Castle, and that is to be followed by an attack on the Castle of Edinburgh. Of course, in taking these fortresses, they expect the coöperation of soldiers within the walls.'

'Splendid!' exclaimed the Captain; 'and what are the generals who are to conduct this grand chain of exploits?'

'Hardie the weaver has been talked about.'

'Hardie!'

'Yes. Perhaps you don't know that he was for some time in the Berwickshire Militia. They expect also to get the services of a weaver named Baird, in the village of Condorret, through which the Radical forces will necessarily march to Carron. Two students have been appointed as chiefs of the medical staff.'

'What students?'

'Young fellows named Macpherson and Dalziel.'

'That's your friend, Andrew, isn't it?'

'That's my friend, Captain, as you say. I wish him all success in the path of glory, and I sincerely trust that he will get a service of Government pills for his pains.'

'What do you mean, Andrew?'

'I mean globules of lead, my good friend Lees; a kind of pill that is generally administered with small doses of a substance composed of saltpetre, sulphur, and charcoal.'

'Well, gentlemen,' said the Captain, 'I thank you for your reports, which are most valuable. A few more meetings, and we shall be done with our work, which is none of the pleasantest, in spite of the consciousness that we may be the means of doing good service to our country in out-generalling an organisation of fools. I need not re-urge upon you to be cautious, nor repeat that your policy is not one of obstruction but of practical facilitation.'

'Our next meeting?' asked King.

'Saturday evening,' answered the Captain.

Captain Batwing sat long after his lieutenants had retired, and brooded profoundly on the reports which he had received. But the Radical proclamation particularly arrested his attention. He pored over it until he had completely mastered its contents; and then, having written a letter, and lighted his inseparable pipe, he lay back in his chair, and once more ascended on clouds of his own making into a still region of romance.

In that region, exhausted by mental anxiety, he fell fast asleep, and when he awoke he saw on the hearthstone the ruins of his pipe. He shuddered, and went to bed with an ominous chill at his heart.

CHAPTER IX.

CARMYLE CASTLE.

PATE FOX, having brooded several days over Campbell's letter, and having consulted Bob Lintie on the subject of it, resolved, on the earnest advice of the latter, to submit the epistle to Lord Carmyle.

'Hae ye ony objections, Bob, to gahg wi' me? I wad like your company.'

'I'm no very strong yet, Pate, and it's a gay bit journey to Carmyle Castle.'

'The walk 'll do ye guid, man, and we'll start early in the afternoon, and tak it easy. Say the word!'

Bob at length consented, with the approval of his wife, who stipulated that they were to be extremely careful, respectful, and not too talkative.

'It's better,' she told them, 'to say less than eneugh than owre muckle, especially to great folk.'

'Nae fear,' answered Pate. 'We hae guid Scotch tongues in our head; but we ken when to begin and when to stop, as weel's onybody.' Then Pate turned to May, and said, 'I wad like to tak' ye wi' us, my bonnie rosebud. The Castle's a sicht I wad like ye to see; but I doubt it's owre far for your wee tender feet to gang and come.'

'Thank ye, Pate; but if ye're gaun to see a lord, I'm gaun to see a leddy.'

'Heth, May, but ye're in luck and wut. I like to hear ye speak sae cheerily. Wha's the leddy, if it's a fair question?'

'A frien' o' your ain—Christine.'

'Eh! weel, ye're richt to ca' her a leddy. There's no mony like her, I'm thinking; and she's better than ever, since her faither lost a' his siller. But it's like faither, like dochter. He paid twenty shillings in the pound, and she's paid the same, if no mair; for she didna lie down and bubble and greet like some I hae seen when fortune left them.'

'I could sit a' day, Pate, and hear ye on that subject,' said Mrs. Annie Lintie; 'and I couldna wish May to hae a better example o' kindness and courage than bonnie Dundas, wha comes and gangs like a sunny licht, aye leaving a blessing ahint her, and never saying a word about it. If it hadna been for her and you, Pate—'

'Nae mair, Anne,' broke in the twister quickly; 'dinna mention my name in the ae breath wi' hers. Yet it's a pleasing thought to think that angels and raggit twisters may work thegither in the same guid cause. Ye're surprised at my words, Anne; but I aye think that kind-hearted women are weel deserving to be ca'd angels. There's your ain May, now, no to mention yoursel'; she's been ane o' my favourite angels since ever she could speak or gang; and mony a time the sicht o' her has saved me frae thoughts that were a gay sicht waur than the blues. Ye canna blush at that, May; your face is a perpetual blush, aye sae bricht and bonnie; and your een!—o'd, May, if I were a young chap, there's no a birkie in Glasgow wad marry ye but mysel'.'

'Gae 'wa', Pate,' said Mrs. Lintie, slapping the twister softly on the shoulder; 'ye're a fine, auld, wise, kind fule o' a man; but May's owre young to think o' sic ferlies.'

'The mair's the pity for me,' replied Pate in a sad voice, but chuckling inwardly.

'But I'm no owre young to like ye, Pate,' said the girl earnestly, as she gave the twister her hand, and looked in his face with eyes that quite brought his heart to his mouth.

'Eh, lass! Bless me, d'ye see that, Anne? Dinna say a word. May's in the richt. It's better to like than to lo'e an auld man; but there's mair love in May's liking than in maist folks' love. My bonnie dearie, ye're the only twister, and ye gar the strings o' my heart twirl just as if a new thread was being twisted to an auld thrum below my breist-bane.'

'Hae ye been tasting the day, Pate?'

'No, Bob. That's to say—'

'O, just sae!'

'That's to say,' continued Pate, 'a' that I hae been tasting is the tipple o' May's een; and though I'm no just fou, I fin' mysel' lifted a wee bittie abin the common level o' things.'

'Clean daft!'

'No sae bad's that, man. But will ye let me finish my sermon? I say, in conclusion—and let nae mither nor faither deny it—that it's out o' sic mouths and een as May's that not only wisdom, but love, is perfected; and there's an end. Guid-day,

dearie, and gie my ither angel a' the weel-wishes
that I haena gien to yoursel'. Come awa, Bob. I'm
quite inspired now, and I hae the courage to meet a
hale battalion o' Radicals, wi' their pokers and tangs,
penny pikes, and roosty sparrow-guns. Guid-day,
Anne!'

'Guid-day, Pate. See and keep steady, baith
gaun and coming; and, for gudesake, try and bridle
your tongue when ye gang up yonder.'

The two men went away laughing. Mrs. Lintie
and her blooming daughter were going westward together. Pate and Bob trudged slowly eastward along
the Gallowgate into the country, towards Carmyle
Castle.

It was the 1st of April, neither warm nor cold,
but bright and fresh, and very pleasant to the two
travellers. To Bob Lintie especially the pure breezes,
that from the fields and the woods brought occasional
breaths of delicate odour, seemed as if sent from
Heaven to give him new life and new hope. But the
walk was supremely interesting to both men, who
retained the power to take delight in simple things.
The air was not only fresh and sweet, but was also
full of music, the odour of the souls of birds. There
seemed to be a lark in every cloud, and every tree
thrilled with melody. The wan weaver and the grizzly
twister were transported quite beyond the kingdom
of heddles and treddles and threads and thrums.

They felt stirring within them those mysterious aspirations, poetic and religious, which, under special
conditions, will sometimes disturb the veriest clods
of humanity. But Pate Fox and Bob Lintie were in
no sense clods. However unskilled they might be
in academic lore and the Fine Arts, they had some
knowledge of the artless art of the spring-birds, the
beauty of the spring-flowers, and the inspiring influences of spring-weather. Pate at length sat down
upon a green hillock, which commanded a partial,
but most suggestive, glimpse of Carmyle Castle
among its fast greening woods, with the brimming
Clyde flowing beneath its antique walls. After gazing
a moment, the twister broke out :

'It beats onything I ever heard or saw !'

'What is't, Pate ?' asked Bob, as he quietly took
a seat beside his companion.

'Did ye ever see sae bonnie a scene, or hear the
birds sing sae sweetly ? O'd it's a braw worl'; and
a sicht like that maks a body wonner how the deevil
the Radicals can think o' cutting ither folks' throats,
and blawing out the brains o' their betters.'

'Maybe it's because they dinna like their betters
to hae what they haena themsels. That's your ain
joke, Pate—d'ye mind ?'

'Ay, ay. That's true o' some o' them at least.'

'Weel, Pate, it really is a bonnie place,' said Bob,
after silently scanning the scene before him. 'I hae

seen 't afore, but never wi' the same pleasure; everything looks sae fine and fresh like, just as if it were
new-made.'

The two sat silent for a few minutes, looking and
listening. Then Bob slipt out his flute, which he
always carried with him, and played some music that
suited the genius of the season. Pate was charmed,
and said so, but demanded a tune of a different kind
from those already played. Bob knew that his friend
was never so well pleased with music as when it made
him sad and brought him to the brink of tears, so
he indulged him with a couple of old Scotch airs of
the most heartrending pathos, which seemed to make
the very birds pause in wonder and the trees to quiver
with ecstasy. In the middle of the second tune Pate
stopped him suddenly by saying,

'Nae mair, Bob, for the love o' gudeness; there's
something in my throat that'll mak me choke—'

'Nay, go on,' said a voice behind them, 'I like
that air, although it wakens unfortunate memories.'

Pate and Bob started to their feet at the sudden
voice, and both in a breath exclaimed,

'My lord!'

It was, indeed, Lord Carmyle himself, who, wandering about the grounds, and attracted by the un-
usual sound of a flute in that locality, had stolen
quietly up behind them.

'Pate Fox the twister!'

'The same, my lord, nae less; and this is my
freen, Bob Lintie, weaver, fiddler, and fluter.'

'Lintie!' said his lordship. 'That's a capital
name for a musician; and it's no flattery, Bob, to
say that you play with soul as well as skill. If you
play the fiddle as well as you play the flute, I should
think that you might put them to some use as a
means of livelihood.'

'And sae I do, my lord,' answered Bob, not in-
sensible to the genial words of his noble critic. 'If
it hadna been for my fiddle and flute, Gude kens
what wad hae come owre us.'

'Then you are not a bachelor, like Pate?'

'No, my lord; I hae a wife and ae bairn.'

'Very good—very good.'

An air of abstraction came into Lord Carmyle's
eyes as he slowly uttered these words, and heaved a
palpable sigh. It seemed as if he was busy with
some thought which time had as yet failed to bury
in the common dust of memory. After a little, he
said:

'But what brings you into this part of the county?
Not idle curiosity, I am sure?'

'No,' said Pate. 'We cam' to see your lordship.'

'Indeed! I am very glad to see you both,
and shall be glad to serve you. Any special business?'

His lordship began to walk towards the castle,
followed by the pair, whom he invited to accompany
him. As they walked along, Pate made answer:

'I hardly ken, my lord, what to say. It's no exactly business we cam' about; but it's maybe important eneugh. The short and the lang o't is that
I hae got frae a freen in Dunkeld a letter that mentions your lordship's name in a way that clean puzzles me. Ye'll maybe laugh at us, my lord, but we
thought it wad do nae harm to let ye read it and
judge for yoursel'.'

'In that ye acted wisely,' his lordship remarked,
smiling, as he took the letter which Pate handed to
him, evidently rather amused than interested. 'If
you will come with me and wait till I have read it,
I shall give you my opinion.'

A few minutes' walking brought them to Carmyle
Castle, which stood on a high bank overlooking the
Clyde, commanding extensive views both up and
down the river. Both banks, as far as could be seen
either way, were wooded to the very edge of the
water, and the eye caught glimpses of cultivated
fields beyond the fringe of the trees. At this point
the Clyde flowed through a natural gorge. But
though the top level of both banks was about equal,
that upon which the castle stood sloped rather steeply
downward, whereas the opposite bank rose from the
river more than two hundred feet in almost perpen-

dicular height. This height was, however, divided in two portions. Half way from the level of the water there occurred a terrace, from which rose a huge wall of rock, having at the foot of it a narrow pathway. Crowning the rock could be seen the remains of an ancient priory, but the ruins were so intermingled with trees, plants, and crawling shrubs, that it was evident that Nature had long since resumed her green sceptre, and lent to the crumbling art of man graces of form and colour which it had not entered into the brain of the original artist to conceive. Behind the priory lay the decayed orchard of the monks, some apple trees remaining; and behind the orchard stood a number of great oaks, very old, and very gnarled, yet not incapable of still withstanding the tempests of many years. Seen from the castle, the priory seemed a perfect nest of beauty; while the castle, seen from priory, looked like an ancient warrior, weather-stained and battle-scarred, and still majestic after centuries of inaction and repose.

As Lord Carmyle, with his two visitors, approached the castle he hailed a servant, whom he instructed to take Pate and Bob to Adam Gordon, the butler.

'And tell Adam,' said his lordship, 'that these travellers are to be entertained as he would entertain himself after a long journey.'

This was done to the letter, for both Pate and

Bob maintained that they had never been better used in their life.

Meanwhile his lordship proceeded to a special room in the north-west angle of the castle, the window of which looked down the Clyde, and began to read Campbell's epistle to Pate.

CHAPTER X.

LORD CARMYLE.

LORD CARMYLE was about fifty. Yet, although he looked all his years, that fact did not seem to arise from the effect of severe occupations like those of the soldier, or from unwise living, which was common enough at that time among the middle and upper classes of society. His figure was tall and still unbent, and he had a commanding air, which was, however, softened by a disposition which seemed more solicitous of admitting and securing the rights of others than in pushing his own claims. The conciliatoriness of his manner, and the tender thoughtfulness of his eye, perhaps rather helped to conceal than to indicate the real depth and strength of his character. Looking at his broad brow, clear eye, and firm lip, a casual observer would have fancied that he was a man who might have taken a high

position among the aristocracy of the country. Nor
would this opinion have been wrong. His lordship
was endowed with good intellectual powers—not
exactly genius, nor merely talent, but qualities that
partook of the nature of both, containing something
of the originality of the one and much of the practical dexterity of the other. Men who knew him,
and had watched his course at the University, concluded in their own minds that young Douglas was
clearly marked out for the career of a statesman.
Their anticipations were well founded, and ought to
have been fulfilled.

But a sudden change passed over the landscape
of his life ; and all the brilliant anticipations of his
friends, and his own more reasonable hopes, seemed
blighted in the bud as by the unseen breath of the
pestilence.

Before the death of his father, the late Lord Carmyle, Sir James Douglas had travelled extensively
in European countries. He returned from the last
of these journeys in 1797 in high hopes, the doors of
Parliament standing wide open before him, leading
to and suggesting the struggles of politicians and
the triumphs of statesmen. But the joy of Sir
James in returning to his native country did not
wholly arise from anticipations of the great public
career that lay before him. He was drawn home by
a sweeter and subtler power. The spirit of love

drew him. He saw in the mirror of his affection the vision of a beautiful girl, his wife by secret contract, and, as he hoped, soon to be his wife by noble public acknowledgment. This it was which gave wings to his imagination, made his heart burn as he crossed the Scottish Border, and put ever new spurs to the sides of his flying steed. The nearer he approached his destination, the more confident grew his hope, the intenser became his affection; and when at length he halted at his inn at Hamilton with the intention of making a special inquiry, and then rush to the arms of his lady, it was in that moment of fond suspense and expectation that three dreadful words were spoken which seemed to him to shake the world.

'*She has vanished!*'

These were the words.

'She has vanished, and no one knows whither. Her mother died with grief through some evil rumour about yourself; then her child was born; and when she was sufficiently recovered, she went away with her infant son and her maid.'

This was the communication which was made to Sir James, and which had the effect of transforming the whole purpose of his life. For months and years he sought for his wife and child in all parts of the country—he set all kinds of agencies afoot, but the search proved in vain. From the date of that sin-

gular and distressing event he was a changed man.
Ambition, which, under favourable circumstances,
might have carried him to many triumphs in public
life, died completely out of him. This result un-
doubtedly proved that Sir James Douglas was not a
perfect man. Grief and misfortune such as his
ought not, and generally do not, destroy, but only
chasten honourable ambition. But, this criticism
allowed, it remains to be said that, though the current of his ideas and aspirations was diverted from
its original channel, his life did not thereby become perverted. He lived henceforth more as a
private gentleman than as a man who might, had he
chosen, have mingled with and taken a conspicuous
part in the social and political life of the nation.
Even when, at his father's death, he became Lord
Carmyle, and had the strongest possible inducements
to reënter the world and take up the broken thread
of his career, little or no change came over his tastes
and predilections. He remained practically a private
man. But he was by no means an inactive one.
His estates absorbed much of his attention. As a
landlord, he acted on the principle which first gives
every possible facility to the tenant, and then looks
in due season for a proper, but neither a fixed nor a
forced return. This principle never failed in his
hands, and, in consequence, he was by far the most
popular landlord in Lanarkshire.

But further, Lord Carmyle was a man of rare benevolence ; though sometimes, it was thought, his charitable deeds assumed very eccentric forms. The truth was, however, that he did not permit his benefactions to flow too much through the recognised channels, but often dispensed them with his own hands, after personal investigation. During the distresses in Glasgow, when Radicalism reared its minatory head, his lordship performed a world of good, of the real authorship of which the world had not the remotest notion.

One of the principal mediums through which he acted in this way was his friend Dr. Thomas Chalmers, to whose schemes of social and educational reform he gave a continuous and powerful support. The Doctor often visited at Carmyle ; and Lord Carmyle was seldom in Glasgow without calling upon the Doctor. Indeed, from the time when the famous preacher settled in Glasgow, his lordship had been one of his most constant friends and supporters.

These slender hints regarding Lord Carmyle's past life must serve the purpose of linking his lordship somewhat definitely to the thread of the narrative.

While Adam Gordon was feasting Pate and Bob with a princely dinner, and while Bob and Pate on the other hand were regaling Adam with music and *wut*, Lord Carmyle was reading the letter the two had brought him. He read it a second time—he

even read it a third time; and parts of it he read a
half-dozen times.

At first his lordship began to read it carelessly,
as if there could not possibly be anything in it to
interest him. Very soon, however, his attention was
continuously fixed upon the document. At one point
he stopped suddenly, and started to his feet, putting
his hand to his head, and feeling his eyes, apparently
for the purpose of ascertaining whether he was sleeping or dreaming, or whether all was right there.
He sat down to it once more, and devoured it line
by line, in an eager and strangely agitated manner.
When it was finished, he lay back in his seat like
one who, having been suddenly stunned, endeavours
to keep together his wandering ideas, and to unite
them to the present and the past in some sort of in-
telligible sequence.

Then he walked through the chamber, his eyes
filled with the mist of confused thought. Looking
from the window of the room, he saw a glorious
stretch of green landscape, through which the river
rolled like a belt of quivering silver. But the sight
simply dazzled him without helping to concentrate
his bewildered ideas. In turning, however, to resume his pacings through the room, his eye fell
upon a veiled picture which hung upon the wall.

That accident was decisive.

He went to the spot, unveiled the picture, when

there gleamed upon him the portrait of a beautiful
girl, of perhaps eighteen or nineteen years. How
fresh the picture seemed ! How perfectly lovely was
the face ! and how tenderly the eyes looked into
those of the beholder ! Lord Carmyle stood fascin-
ated before it, with very tears in his eyes. 'O Margaret !' he murmured, 'how like a dream does all
the past appear, with those eyes looking into mine,
as they were wont to do in the warmth and loveliness of life !' Rousing himself with a painful effort
from the trance of tender and tragic recollections
into which he was drifting, he rang a bell, saying,
as he did so, 'The mystery that surrounds these
poor women must be unravelled. Perhaps—yes, it
may be that they know something of old times—of
our sad story, and the sad secret of it;' and as his
lordship spoke, his eyes were fixed earnestly on the
portrait. His own face was a picture of hope and
determination, yet touched with a palpable shade of
despair.

When an attendant appeared, he made him show
up Pate Fox, who in two minutes stood in the
middle of the room, bowing, as best he could, to his
noble friend.

'Sit down, Pate,' said his lordship, also taking a
seat ; 'I have read the letter, which seems to me
both curious and important. Could you let it remain with me a short time ?'

'As lang's ye like, my lord.'

'To be open with you, Pate, my object is to try by every means to find out the history of the two poor women mentioned by your friend Campbell, and I want you to take his advice, and watch for them.'

'I'm quite willing to do that; but it puzzles me how to gang about it. I dinna ken them, and there's nae saying when they may come, and they mayna come to Glasgow ava, but gang to Hamilton, as Jamie says in the letter.'

'That is true; and I admit that your seeing them at all is a mere chance. Still, you can keep your eyes open. There is one mark that may guide you.'

'What's that?'

'The circumstance that they are *two*. There is another thing. If they have walked all the way, they must be footsore and fearfully worn and weary.'

'Weel, my lord, that maks it mair possible to ken them. I'll keep my een about me.'

'Do so; and get your friend Lintie to do the same. Should you be so fortunate as to find them, though it is a remote chance indeed, persuade them, if you can, either to come to me or to stay with Lintie till you can inform me. If they left Dunkeld at the time Campbell mentions, they must be near their journey's end.'

'Then the sooner we're awa the better,' said
Pate, rising; 'this is Saturday, and I have aye observed that a gay wheen queer things tak' place on
that day.'

'Thank you, Pate. I shall make similar arrangements at Hamilton, so that we may have a
double chance of discovering who these women are.
But, Pate, you and Lintie will do me the further
favour of keeping this matter dark in the mean
time.'

'That will we, nae fear. Gude guide us!' exclaimed the twister, as his eye caught the portrait
on the wall, ' wha's picture's that ?'

'The portrait of an early friend of mine,' said his
lordship in a low voice.

'Weel, that beats a'.'

'What do you see in it, Pate, that makes you
speak so ?'

'It's no the beauty o't, my lord, though it's as
bonnie a face as I ever saw, except, maybe, a freen
o' mine down in Glasgow. What surprised me sae
muckle at first was to see how close it resembles a
young acquaintance o' yours and mine. If he had
a sister, I wad say that was her very looking picture.'

'Whom do you mean ?' asked his lordship with
some curiosity.

'Alan Dalziel.'

Lord Carmyle gave an imperceptible start, looked
eagerly at the portrait, then at Pate, and then sank
into a profoundly thoughtful mood. There was silence in the room for the space of five minutes, and
the only sound that reached the twister's ear was the
voices of some birds sitting on a high ledge of the
castle, and doubtless in serious confabulation as to
the propriety of building certain nests for the purpose of consummating certain marriages. Pate's eye
also caught that lovely stretch of the Clyde to which
we have already referred, admired it very much, and
wished that May Lintie had been present with him
to see it. At length, as his lordship began to finger
among some papers, the twister said,

'Weel, my lord, I maun be gaun.'

'One moment, Pate. I owe you something.'

'Do you, my lord?'

'That is to say, I hope so.'

'I should hae hoped sae too, but I'm feared ye're
wrang.'

'Then I suppose that you did not preserve the
guinea I gave you two years ago in the Gallowgate?'

Pate shook his head as he replied:

'It's no easy for folk like me to keep siller.'

'I should think not. But how did it go?—not
into the stoup, I hope.'

'No, my lord, thank gudeness! I've maist cured
mysel' o' that bad habit.'

'Well, but tell how it disappeared. You will recollect that there was a sort of compact over the destiny of that bit of gold.'

Pate hesitated; but seeing that it would be better to be open with his lordship, he replied:

'If ye hadna speer't, my lord, I wad ne'er hae tell't ye; but as ye hae a richt to ken, I maun just say that I gied the first hauf o't to Mrs. Campbell when Jamie was in prison; and the ither hauf I gied to my auld acquentance Jock Makane, when he gaed awa to America. That's the history o' the guinea, my lord, as true as death.'

'I believe you, Pate; and let me tell you that you have made a better use of it than I bargained for. It puts me in mind of the parable of the talents; and I feel myself in honour bound to follow out the parable to the honest end.'

'Ne'er fash your heid, my lord.'

'There is nothing like keeping to the letter, Pate, in a case like this. If I am not to be true with you, it would be worse than bankruptcy. Inasmuch as you employed the one guinea I gave so profitably, I now give you five sovereigns. See how fine they look— they are newly coined.'

'Five sovereigns! And what am I to do wi' them?'

'I can trust you to use them well.'

'Ye're owre kind, my lord; and yet I'm very

thankfu'. Bob Lintie has been lang no weel, and he and his wife and bonnie wee dochter May are gay ill aff the now; sae I'll be able to pay back some o' their kindness to me.'

'They are good people these Linties, I suppose?' said his lordship thoughtfully.

'Nane mair sae, my lord; and I should ken.'

'In that case, Pate, I shall intrust with you these five for Bob, which will help him and his family till he is fully recovered. But keep it all quiet, remember.'

'My lord,' said Pate, after a pause of intense admiration, 'ye put me in mind o' a remark Mr. Dundas made about ane like yoursel'.'

'Mr. Dundas is a bit of a Radical, isn't he?'

'Ay, that he is; but he's a Radical wi' a difference.'

'Indeed. What difference?'

'Common sense; and it's for the want o' that they're a' gaun pell-mell to the deil again. But the remark o' Mr. Dundas was this: he was speaking about a person o' title and guidness like yoursel', when he said that the stroke o' the King's pen made him a lord, but it was God Almichty that made him a man.'

'Or, in other words, as our Poet says, a king can make a belted knight; but the creation of an honest man is beyond the royallest art. Sound philosophy.

But what about the Dundas family? I heard of their
trouble. Is Christine as fair as ever? And is young
Dalziel still faithful, in spite of adversity?'

'A' things are gaun weel wi' Lewis, my lord.
His trouble didna trouble him muckle. That he was
able to pay a' his debts was eneugh for honour,
though he hadna a bawbee left for necessity. The
very house that his faither built had to gang wi' the
rest; and they were forced to flit; but they did sae
as if they had won a battle. I never saw onything
like it. And the young leddy—I mean Christine—
instead o' being cast down into a sea o' dispair, because she was made tocherless in the clap o' a haun,
never drapped a tear the mair o't; or if she did, it
wasna for hersel', but for her parent, made penniless
after sae many years o' honest and honourable work
and weeldoing. But as ae door steeks anither opens.
Lewis was soon snappit up by a gentleman, wha kent
the value o' his lear and skill.'

'And young Dalziel?' said Lord Carmyle, as
Pate made a pause.

'O, he's weel eneugh; and I'm gien to believe
that the courtship o' him and Christine still hauds
guid. Alan was owre sensible a chap to let sae
bonnie and sae guid a lass slip through his fingers
because ill-fortune had the cheek to pick her pouch.
Nae fortune could be equal to hersel'—at least, sae
is my opinion. But for ane sae wise-like, Alan's gay

foolish too, especially considering that he has only himsel' to depend on.'

'But how is he foolish?'

'Wad ye believe it! he's got mixed up wi' thae Radicals again.'

'And they appear to mean real mischief this time.'

'Sae it seems. But I'm gay far cheated if the authorities dinna mean to gie them full value for their bad siller.'

'That is the fact, Pate. If they once commit themselves, I fear the foolish men won't be allowed to escape without some signal punishment. It is melancholy to think of it. Do you ever see Alan?'

'Only at an anterin time; but he never escapes without getting a guid bit o' my mind. He hasna the excuse o' gaun to ruin blin'. But forgie me, my lord, I'm taking up owre muckle o' your time.'

'Well, Pate, good-bye; and remember what we were talking about.'

'Depend on me, my lord,' said the twister confidently, as he walked away, not unlike a Providence in rags.

As Pate and Bob reached the main road, they heard the clatter of a horse's feet coming from the direction of the Castle. Looking back, they saw Lord Carmyle, who waved his hand to them, riding at a great pace in the direction of Hamilton.

CHAPTER XI.

MORE HINTS OF DESTINY.

WE must follow Lord Carmyle for a few minutes.

When he fairly reached the highway, he gave the rein to the splendid mare he rode, his famous Cora Linn, who, taking the well-known hint, leapt into the wind, and in less than fifteen minutes devoured the five miles of space which stretched between Carmyle Castle and the town of Hamilton.

In two minutes more his lordship was sitting in the office of his lawyers, Archer and Son. Young Archer was alone.

'Your father is not better?'

'Worse, my lord; and I fear he will never be able to visit the office again.'

'That is unfortunate. I wished to consult him about a particular affair.'

'Could I not serve you, my lord? My father has made me fully acquainted with your affairs to the minutest detail. He did this to provide against contingencies.'

Lord Carmyle hesitated, but only for a moment. He then asked:

'Did he recount to you that strange event—that mystery?'

'Yes, my lord; I know it thoroughly; and, to

tell you the truth, it has recently absorbed much of my thought. It is one of those circumstances which fascinate me. Hitherto, my father would not permit me to think of it; but I have often wondered whether, late as it is, it would not be possible to discover some clue to the mystery. If it were not disagreeable to yourself—'

'Stop a minute, William. Before you go any farther, be so good as read that letter, and tell me what you think of it. The person to whom it is addressed brought it to-day, partly, as you will see, in obedience to an injunction in the letter itself, and partly from an impression of his own that it might be of some value.'

William Archer read and re-read Campbell's letter, very carefully both times, and then, after a little reflection, said:

'My belief is, my lord, that the matter of this epistle may be of the utmost importance. I am the more inclined to think so from a circumstance which I must hint to you. Some time ago, an acquaintance intrusted me with a peculiar commission. It was, if possible, to make a discovery, the nature of which I need not state in the mean time. At first the affair seemed entirely hopeless, and necessarily the inquiries I made brought me into contact with strange people and circumstances. Moreover, the scope of these inquiries led me a number of years

into the past. One of the suggestions I got to begin
with was the name of a person mentioned in this
very letter—Hawk; and the same person intersected
various points of my line of investigation. What is
more singular, I have traced this man into some
mysterious connection with Sir John Home.'

'Sir John Home?'

'Yes, my lord, Sir John Home, who is,' added
the young lawyer somewhat deliberately, 'your cousin
and heir.'

Lord Carmyle paused, greatly puzzled over this
new fact. It seemed strange that Sir John should
have any special connection or intercourse with a
man like this Hawk. Still, his lordship was not
ignorant of the less favourable features of his cousin's
character; and he thought it not unlikely that these
two, so different in social position, might have reasons for meeting each other of a kind which—although neither would care to publish them to the
world — might yet be innocent enough in a legal
point of view. Sir John, his lordship thought, was
too much of a lawyer to commit himself with a man
of doubtful character.

'Your opinion of Sir John is perhaps correct,
my lord,' said Archer; 'it is certainly more favourable than mine. This Hawk appears to be the leader
of a band of gipsies; but I don't think that he has
always been so, and I feel profoundly convinced of

two things regarding the connection between the
Baronet and him.'

'Do they affect this investigation?'

'Very materially. I believe that their connection
is not only evil, but criminal; and that part, if not
the whole of it, has reference to these poor women
whose names—or rather nicknames—are mentioned
in this curious letter.'

'But the grounds of your belief?'

'They are curious, my lord. In the course of
my inquiries I found that Bonnington of the Duke's
Arms had a profound suspicion and dislike of Sir
John Home. This was very interesting to me—too
interesting not to be probed and solved. Well, after
much hesitation on his part, Bonnington confided to
me what he called his "religious conviction," that
Sir John was somehow mixed up with, if he was not
the cause of, that mysterious disappearance so many
years ago.'

'Why, Archer, this must be some romance, or
Bonnington is a fool.'

Yet Lord Carmyle, in spite of this remark, became very thoughtful. It was evident, too, that this
peculiar allusion to his old overwhelming woe saddened and pained him.

'It may be a romance, my lord,' replied Archer,
'but I should like to discover personally whether it
is so. As to Bonnington being a fool, I must just

say that he is not therefore disabled from being a witness—from bearing sound testimony to a fact.'

' If the fact exists.'

' Precisely. Well, my impression is that Bonnington is not a fool, and that his suspicions are, therefore probably based on something real — although I confess that he has never been able to define clearly the reasons of his dislike and doubt. But I think I can perceive one of the reasons. Bonnington says that this man Hawk and Sir John were in frequent confabulation about the time of that distressing affair, and that immediately it occurred the gipsy disappeared from the neighbourhood, and was not seen for a whole year. When he reappeared, Sir John and he met in the Duke's Arms, where they held a long secret conference. Similar conferences took place several years running, and then they stopped. But Bonnington believes that the meetings of Hawk and Sir John were nevertheless continued elsewhere.'

' But is there any proof of this ?'

' The probability of it is proved by a fact. Sir John and his gipsy friend met again in February last in the Duke's Arms. This time, however, their conference was not altogether secret.'

' How was that ? Was there a third party ?'

' There was a third party. The fact is, the mission with which I was intrusted by my friend war-

ranted me in having the two gentlemen watched—
keyholed, as I may say. Unfortunately, they carried
on their conversation in so careful a tone, that only
snatches of it were audible. Enough, however, was
caught to justify my conclusions that the connection
of these men has something to do with Nightingale
and Swallow, the women named in this letter, and
that, in some way, there is an element of crime
in it. It appears, moreover, that the compact between them, or whatever it is, is approaching a
crisis.'

Archer paused; and Lord Carmyle sat clouded
with thought, his mind evidently busy with many
things. At length he remarked:

'It is a curious story, Archer, and there may be
something in the intercourse of these two men which
you and I would not care to defend; but it is far from
being clear that their conduct would justify Bonnington's suspicion. It is too horrible.'

'But not impossible—horrible as its truth would
be. You can see at least how the suspicion was en-
gendered in Bonnington's mind.'

'Yes; the facts you state cannot easily be got
rid of. But how do they affect your special investigations?'

'Well, I have only discovered proof of what I
knew or suspected before. Unless I can compel
either Hawk, or one of the two women to speak

and honestly confess all they know, I shall fail. But
this letter may help us.'

'Yes,' said his lordship eagerly, 'it is about
it that I wish to consult you. Thinking that the
two poor women mentioned in it may know something which might help to unravel the old mystery,
it has struck me that it would be advisable to secure
them before they fall again into the hands of Hawk
—for I feel assured that he will hunt them down, if
they know a single fact which he wishes to conceal.
What do you think?'

Archer did not answer at once, although Lord
Carmyle's remarks seemed to rouse him more
thoroughly to the importance of the situation.

'My lord,' he said at length, 'it is most essen-
tial that we should endeavour to find these women.
But we can't force them; our policy must be to in-
duce them to make revelations.'

'If Campbell's letter is correct in representing
them as having been detained by Hawk against their
will, they can hardly refuse to speak.'

'I think not—if we only had them.'

'That is the question now. I have set two men
to watch for them at Glasgow, and I want you to do
the same here in case they should come to Hamilton.'

'I accept the charge, and I shall take care that
they do not escape. But there is one thing, my
lord—'

'Well?'

'Pardon me if I seem too bold; but I must suggest the propriety of watching the motions of Sir John for a few days.'

'For what purpose? You don't really credit Bonnington's suspicions?'

'I don't quite know. I am in a condition of doubt — I neither believe nor disbelieve. While hoping that they are false, I can't avoid the view that they are possibly true. If they are true,' Archer added, in a low yet penetrating voice, 'Sir John is the only person who could profit by their truth.'

'You amaze me!' said Lord Carmyle, pale and astonished; 'what are you really driving at?'

'The statement of a single fact, my lord, will reveal my drift. At one time there seemed a hope — nay, a certainty — of maintaining the Carmyle estates in the direct line of succession. That hope and that certainty were suddenly destroyed, and—'

'What then?'

'Sir John Home is now your only heir.'

'Archer, you are merciless!'

His lordship sat like death, brooding over the young lawyer's daring suggestion, which pointed to the probable commission of some frightful crime.

'Not merciless, my lord, but logical. In a case involving so many uncertainties and singularities, if we are to arrive at a full disclosure of the truth, it can only be by assuming in the mean time the truth of the worst probability.'

When Lord Carmyle took his leave, Archer remained in his office about ten minutes, during which he had arranged his plan of operations. He also wrote a note to Alan Dalziel, and sent it off by special messenger. Then he muttered to himself:

'If my calculations and speculations are not absolutely false, I feel that I am on the brink of a discovery which will astonish my Lord Carmyle even more than the proved villany of his smooth cousin and heir. And, Alan, my friend, if you too don't share in the astonishment, I shall bury my books in the Avon and become the Hermit of Haughhead.'

Haughhead was the name of the place where Archer lived.

Lord Carmyle rode home in a strange state of mental turbulence and distress. When he reached Bothwell Bridge the sun was going down, clear and beautiful. All the west was one flush of tender gold, and the flowing river was paved with the rosy radiance. The fresh budding woods were also smitten with the delicate spring light, which seemed even to touch the souls of the birds and inspire them with sweeter and happier melodies. As the rider paused and looked down the river, he remembered that nearly twenty-three years ago he stood on the same spot.

But it was then the sad and silent autumn of the year, and now it was the melodious spring.

Then, the great cloud of his life had fallen upon him, and he felt that he was a blasted man. Now, after all these years of sorrow and suffering, when he had long given up all hope of ever being able to unveil the mystery of that awful blow, was it possible that he was about to have his memory more profoundly darkened by learning all the evil depth of the calamity?

CHAPTER XII.

THE NIGHT ANGEL.

THE night was starry and beautiful, as the angel of the still watches floated once more in mid-air.

With her fine penetrating eye, she saw the river flowing from the rich vales and bosky woods of Lanarkshire, leaping like a silver sword from a green scabbard, and severing the city in twain at a single flash. She saw the twinkling lights that, like earthly galaxies and constellations, faintly defined the streets and squares beneath her; and she saw curling upwards the smoke of thousands of happy and unhappy hearths.

From some quarters she heard sounds of music and gladsome din, but the sounds that predominated were not those of comfort and content. There floated to her ear sighs of sadness and words of lamentation. Over her hungry children hung many a tortured mother, her own hunger abolished by the suffering she beheld. Many a father, labourless and penniless, already reckless and growing more desperate at sight of his desolate household, became politically mad, and joined in the plots that were moving onwards to their final plunge.

But the rich and official people of the city, advised by Captain Batwing, were daily and nightly putting their heads together and preparing for the expected event.

By and by the sadness which filled the face of the gentle night angel suddenly cleared away. Her gaze was fixed on the banks of the river.

What did she see there?

Christine Dundas had been to visit a friend at Rutherglen in the afternoon, and Alan Dalziel had gone to fetch her home. Alan had not seen Christine for three days, and he was therefore impatient to be with her, to see her face, to hear her speak, and to touch her hand.

He had his wish. They spent three happy hours

together in Rutherglen. They walked in lovely rustic
gardens; through winding by-lanes that were sweet
with new buds; and along the edges of fields over
which silent waves of tender green seemed to be
rising from invisible regions to the music of simple
birds. Then they walked to the top of a hill which
overlooked the city, and commanded a fine stretch
of scenery across the gentle undulations of Renfrew-
shire to the west, and to the north across Dumbar-
tonshire, where they saw the rugged giants of the
Highlands standing grimly up, the grand bulk of
Benlomond holding them all in solemn subjection.

Yet although all the incidents of the afternoon
were apparently full of pleasure to both the lovers,
Alan, nevertheless, felt that there was something in
the air of Christine which did not completely har-
monise with his own feelings, with the scene around
them, or even with their talk. But the truth is,
what Alan fancied was a cloud in the air of Christine was mostly the reflex of a cloud in his own
mind. It is a common form of illusion for a man
out of harmony with himself to imagine that it is
other people, even his dearest friends, who are out
of harmony with him.

Why was Alan out of harmony with himself?

In recent interviews with Mr. Dundas, the latter
had descanted with remarkable freedom on the blind
folly of the Radical policy, and showed, without

seeming to do so, that he was well acquainted with
their secret meetings, secret drillings, and even with
some of their proposed operations. This staggered
Alan not a little, and he wondered how Mr. Dundas
had acquired his information. Mr. Dundas's object
was to detach Alan from any active connection with
the Radicals. In this he apparently failed. Alan
was, however, really so much affected by the arguments of his friend, the father of Christine, that he
began to feel, if not to see, that perhaps he ought
to throw over the Radicals—so far, at least, as their
secret machinations were concerned. But, then, his
honour was engaged to them; and the influence of
his student-companions, especially of Macpherson,
was so great that he felt totally unable to emanci-
pate himself. Indeed, he was not quite sure whether
he actually wished to do so. He was whirled about
by many winds—political opinions and private de-
sires. He saw so much misery in the city, a large
portion of it, as he imagined, directly attributable to
an evil system of government; and he had drunk so
deeply at the Radical fountains of inspiration that,
in spite of his growing knowledge and the subtler
promptings and suggestions issuing from the beauty
and known opinions of Christine, he could not wholly
divest himself of the belief that the Radical position
was one of high and heroic duty. Yet, in profounder
moments, he thought that he saw in it something

like folly, evil, and danger. But, then, five minutes
in the company of Macpherson banished all cowardly
caution and doubt. No metaphysical cobweb could
withstand for a moment the Celtic intensity of that
stalwart Reformer.

Thus it came that Alan was out of harmony with
himself; and thus it came, also, that even while enjoying, amid the fresh young beauty of spring, the
bright and happy converse of Christine, he vaguely
imagined that there was something strange in her
manner, when it was mainly his own mind that was
clouded and disordered. Somewhere in his consciousness there existed, or was beginning to exist, a
feeling that jarred with his present thoughts; or was
it some new thoughts that jarred with his old feelings? Perhaps that was the true state of the case,
if thought is to be regarded as the creator of that
light which enables a man to distinguish things that
are spiritually incompatible and mutually destructive.

Why should a young man, with all the world before him, and loving so beautiful a maiden, entertain
thoughts of conspiracy and rebellion?

Surely a fair question.

Yet why should a young man, with a reasonable
soul, shirk the grandest of political or human duties,
the liberation of a starved and down-trodden people,
for the love of the fairest of Eve's daughters?

These are the questions that tortured the spirit of

the poor, indecisive, and generous lover—fatherless, motherless, relationless Alan—student of anatomy, chemistry, *materia medica*, and what not, with a little Latin, and less Greek, peripatetic philosopher, night-hawking Radical, and pike-wielding rebel to be.

Well might the angel of the still watches turn her curious benign visage upon the lovers as they wandered slowly homeward along the soft-flowing Clyde towards the dim lamp-flickering city. The angel listened.

'It was good of you, Christine, and brave too, to visit the poor woman.'

'I don't know that it deserves to be called either good or brave. We were told that her baby was dying, and that the family were in sore distress.'

'But what a dismal place to enter, with fever raging in the locality! If you could trust me, I would gladly save you from unnecessary exposure.'

'I have no fear, Alan. Besides, you know, women prefer to see a woman in certain cases of distress.'

'You should remember, though, that I am something of a doctor now; and doctors are never out of place where there is disease.'

'Doctors are useful creatures; but they are not all like Dr. Bannatyne, with his beautiful ways and kindly words.'

'Or Dr. Plato,' said Alan. 'I have seldom seen

a man whose voice and eye are so marvellously me-
dicinal. He cures not by drugs, but by a word, a
touch of the hand, a smile. I suppose the child
died, Christine?'

'Yes,' she replied almost inaudibly; 'and I think
that its death came as much by want as by disease.
Poor little thing, how lean and pinched it was! But
they were all the same. The mother—God pity her!
—what suffering she must have endured! And when
I was there the father came in—a strange sight. So
thin and sharp, with deep-sunk eyes filled with a
fearful light. At first he hardly seemed to care about
the death of his child. Does misery kill affection?
When he spoke, it was not in tones of sorrow, but of
rage and denunciation. He must be a Radical.'

'How so?'

'Because the Government and all constituted authorities seemed alike detestable to him; and if words
could slay, they would all be dead. But he muttered
something about their not being allowed to escape so
easily this time; and though I am not a coward, the
wicked glare that was in his eye, as he spoke about
pikes and muskets, made me shudder. What could
he mean, Alan? Are all the things true that we hear
from day to day?'

These were the questions that Alan expected, yet
shuddered to hear from the lips of Christine; and
the very angel that hung over them veiled her face

when she heard the words. They were drawing near to the city as Alan replied with hesitation, cold at heart:

'I suppose that some of the rumours may be true. But, Christine,' he added pleadingly, 'let us avoid that subject. The discussion of it has always marred our peace.'

'You know, Alan, and know well, that I do not like discord. But tell me, is it possible to keep the peace, or maintain mutual respect and affection, except by openness and a fair understanding? I have hitherto said little to you on the subject; but secretly it has given me more anxiety and pain than you can imagine. You remember what a sad business it was before when you got mixed up with the Radicals. No good was done to the country; and personally you were almost ruined. It is only two years since then, yet I feel as if I had grown ten years older. I see many things in a different, and I think in a clearer, light. Above all things, I see more clearly, and feel more deeply, the wrong and the folly which the poor Radicals are again threatening to commit.'

'Wrong and folly!' said Alan, surprised, and perhaps slightly exasperated.

'How otherwise can you describe their conduct? Everything they want ought perhaps to be granted; though I doubt it. But even if they had a clear right to all they claim, is it anything but folly to

force it in the manner they are threatening to do?
It is folly, because they are utterly unfit to compel
the Government. They can only injure the cause
they wish to serve, and draw vengeance and suffering
upon themselves and families.'

Alan, more surprised and gloomy than ever,
glanced quickly at Christine as they walked along.
He was beginning to feel hot, and there was some
danger that he might lose his temper. This he
knew, and he tried to speak coolly; but his words
were nevertheless injudicious. He only said:

'I doubt, Christine, if women-folk can understand
these questions.'

'Like you men, Alan, we can think that we
understand them. And if we are ignorant, it is
because you neglect or refuse to take us into your
confidence. But my complaint is deeper than that.
Here are we two, with—O, Alan, pardon me for being so plain—here are we two with a lifetime before
us. What should be our aim? Surely, to be open,
trust each other, and work in harmony for our mutual
good. Your own prospects are excellent just now;
why should you endanger them? Why should you
provoke the ruin that almost crushed you before?'

'I am not afraid of ruin,' said Alan sullenly,
rather shirking than answering Christine's attack;
'a nobody like me can't be ruined.'

'Alan!'

'You talk about trusting each other. Is it not clear that you are distrusting me?'

'Not your heart, Alan; not your goodness of purpose; but your judgment, your—'

'My judgment! Well, that's complimentary!'

'Do not mistake me, Alan,' she replied, in a tone of distress. 'I mean that for months you have been mixing with these Radicals and lending them your support; and yet you have concealed everything. Is it possible for me not to feel anxious? Can you not understand how I feel, knowing what we are to each other? Everything looks black and ominous, and I can see nothing but ruin, if you continue to keep company with the conspirators.'

'Be quiet!' he said, with harsh emphasis, as one or two persons passed and looked at them. 'You mean well, Christine; but your interference in this business can't do any good. I have told you nothing; yet you seem to know something about it and me. You must, therefore, have been inquiring of somebody else. Is that fair? Am I a boy, to be watched and held in leading-strings? It does not look respectful; it is scarcely honest.'

The angel that hovered over them in the air still more closely muffled her sorrowful face as these bitter and disastrous words reached her ear.

'O, Alan!' Christine murmured, pale and giddy under the blow of her lover's desperate language.

More talk followed; but it was not an improve-
ment upon the foregoing. Christine endeavoured to
soothe Alan into a better condition of mind; but he
would not be soothed. She tried to convince him that
she was anxious only for his good; but he continued
bitterly unresponsive to her pleading; and at last, in
a fit almost of despair, she made another effort to
show him the folly of rebel Radicalism; but he repelled her arguments with a logic that was almost
brutal in its force.

The angel wrapt herself in a cloud, and wept.

In going through the streets towards home, Christine saw the lights flicker faintly and far away; and
the people that passed close to her seemed like ghosts
gliding soundlessly along.

When they reached home, Alan did not go in
with her. He was still wicked; and they parted
coldly, silently, and as souls that might never meet
again.

CHAPTER XIII.

CLOUDS.

ALL that night the meek-eyed angel continued
to float watchfully over the city, seeing very curious
sights.

. She saw Christine, distraught and with trembling feet, enter her own dwelling. Mr. Dundas and Miss Walkingshaw looked eagerly at her, and knew that something was wrong. For only a few minutes, however, did she linger beside them; and having kissed her father, she stumbled to her own room, followed by Miss Walkingshaw, to whom, with some tears and much distress, she confided the cause of her unhappiness. The kindly, motherly woman soothed and comforted Christine with much tact and tenderness. She contrived to assure her to some extent that Alan's good sense would soon come to his aid, and that all would yet be well.

To say the truth, however, Miss Walkingshaw had some doubts about Alan. She willingly acknowledged whatever good sense he seemed to possess; but she did not fail to perceive that he had not reached any definite mental condition; that he was still intellectually nebulous, suspended in the air, so to speak, and waiting the settlement of questions which only experience, often dearly bought, can effectually settle. In the mean time, both Miss Walkingshaw and Mr. Dundas, while discussing Alan privately, had been compelled to admit to themselves that he would naturally commit many curious mistakes, and that, probably, some such incident as a quarrel between the lovers would occur sooner or later. Never yet has the course of true love run smooth in this world. These two

knew it; so that they were not at all surprised at
this lovers' quarrel, though they were none the less
touched by the piteous plight that Christine seemed
to be in. Moreover, although they expected that this
little cloud would disappear in the sunshine of renewed affection, they augured no good from the Radical movement, and dreaded that some stain might
come to Alan through his connection with it.

Christine, after Miss Walkingshaw left her, lingered long before retiring to rest. Her mind was
tossed by the most tragic apprehensions, and her
heart was torn, as the hearts of young maidens will
be, by feelings and emotions of which no spirit under
the shoulder of Shakespeare could give any perfect
analysis. She was a piteous sight to see, as she
hung in silent agony over the idea of what had taken
place between her and Alan as they walked home by
the river. She blamed herself for being so outspoken;
and yet her judgment was too strong and clear to
allow her to think that Alan was not to blame in
letting himself be borne away by political feeling into
the Radical whirlpool, the growing volume of which
was ringing and raging every day more fearfully in
the ears of the citizens. Clasping her hands, as if
in prayer, she tried to wrestle down her prophetic
fears. The battle was long, and not quite successful.
Christine had much of her father's strength of character; but it was interfused and refined by the sweet-

ness and tenderness of her German mother; so that
her power of thought and will was to some extent
neutralised by her intensity of feeling, which had the
effect of extending the mental conflict.

At length, however, through sheer effort from
the pain of thought, she wearied, became drowsy,
a very dream of beauty, and fell asleep, slowly and
fitfully, as a rose, lately blown and tossed by a tempest, closes its loveliness under the consoling stillness of the stars.

Alan walked home to his lodgings in College-
street in a very unhappy and tempestuous mood.
He thought it strange that Christine should have
assailed him as she did; and he went through a
lengthened and ingenious process of reasoning, in
the attempt to justify the manly and decisive stand
he had made against the interference with projects
that surpassed feminine understanding and experience. But this attempt on Alan's part was altogether unsuccessful. His indignation approved his
logic, but his heart began to whisper that his indignation was a wicked spirit, and was no judge of logic.
In fact, the more Alan cooled down the more miserable he became; and long before he began to think
of going to bed he was feasting on the anguish which
he had so ruthlessly won in repelling and beating
down the pleading of his better angel.

William Archer's note was lying on his table

when he went in. He just glanced at the outside of it, and when he saw the handwriting he tossed his head contemptuously and said,

'Another failure, I suppose. What is the use of making any further inquiry about a father and mother that — psha! I shall write to Archer to spend no more time in the ridiculous search.'

At once he sat down and wrote a wild note to his lawyer friend in Hamilton, which would, had he received it, have considerably astonished the young lawyer. Having sealed and addressed this epistle, Alan sat awhile longer, biting his quill to pieces, and trying to look into the infinite through the roof. The attempt was not satisfactory; and he wriggled himself into all sorts of postures, but could find no cushion for his soul to rest upon. Then, in a fit of caprice, he took up Archer's note, opened and read it for the first time. It was very brief, and ran thus:

'My DEAR ALAN,—Just two lines to say that I have found what seems to be a favourable clue to our mystery. If I don't mistake, too, it will impinge upon another mystery of a most singular character. Of course, nothing is certain; but I may venture now to bid you hope. In case, however, my expectations may be over - sanguine, keep quiet in the mean time, and say nothing about the matter to anybody.

'Love to the loveliest lady in the county. In
spite of your halfpenny misfortunes, you are the
luckiest fellow I know. Only give *me* Christine, and
I shall give you all I have. But you are too wise.
It puzzles me to account for your luck.'

This note was a slight surprise to Alan, and
made him in the first place destroy the one he had
written to Archer. Then he felt that his friend's
praise of Christine was very sweet, and yet very bitter. It was pleasant to know that her beauty dazzled
a judge like Archer; but that knowledge only deepened the bitterness of the feeling produced by his
quarrel with her. This bitterness, however, was not
repentance. It was a mixture of remorse and rage
—the latter as yet predominating.

Alan paused over Archer's statement about the
clue to the mystery.

'Can it be possible?' he thought; 'and who are
they, if they are still living? He bids me hope.
Would he do so if he thought they were nobodies?
Yet he guards me against the hope of complete success by bidding me in a sort of way not to be surprised at failure. His expectations may be over-
sanguine! So they may. Indeed, I doubt they will;
and I fear that this note is like as many others—a
delusion and a snare. The mystery, I fear, will
never be solved.'

So he flung the note down, took up a book, and tried to read. This was a failure, and he pitched the volume into a corner, and walked restlessly through his very small chamber.

The angel of the night - watches still hovered over the city, sad, yet indignant—sad, that two loving hearts should be estranged by causes which were sweeping in ever-widening circles, and would finally crush the simple and the unwary; indignant, that those in power were allowing the tempest to grow and gather, when they might have arrested it in its initial stages, and thus prevented volumes of suffering, and the triple tragedy in which it ended.

There were many curious meetings that night in Glasgow, which the watchful angel witnessed with stern visage. Lord Provost Monteith and lesser officials met in secret conclave, discussed the situation, and made preparations of a civil and military kind, for events which they expected to occur immediately.

Captain Batwing glided through the city alone, but now and again encountering some of his special friends, with whom he seemed to confer in a hurried and stealthy manner. They were particularly interested in watching certain other men, who seemed rather curiously engaged. Two or three of these latter would issue from an entry near the corner of a street, look eagerly about, and then advance and plaster a conspicuous part of the wall with a hand-bill. This done, they would swiftly dart back to their former hiding-place, and issue from it by another way. In all the principal parts of the city this process was repeated with the same watchful precautions. Captain Batwing hovered about and flitted here and there until the dawn. It looked as if he had been weaving a spell which was finished only when the first streak of day was woven into it.

But furthermore, the sad-eyed angel saw a number of messengers take their departure from the city by various roads in the early part of the night. The destinations of these men were the different villages round about Glasgow, and some of them were not reached till midnight. But in all cases, nevertheless, the messengers were received as if they had been expected by persons who had not gone to bed, and in some cases by groups of half-a-dozen. Then very quickly and stealthily the village street-corners were posted with hand-bills like those which were put up in the city.

All these sights, and the meaning which lay under them, had made sadder and sterner the benignant brows of the spirit that hovered unweariedly in the air. Now, however, as she turned her eyes towards the north-east, her face became suddenly luminous with the light of divine pity and hope.

What did she see ?

Only two poor women, many miles away, coming towards the city; but O, so slowly, slowly, wearily, wearily, footsore and heartsore, and pursued by the shadow of a great fear.

Why did they not seek shelter from the darkness and the coldness of the night?

Looking farther towards the north, the angel saw the reason, and became terrible as the spirit of vengeance. The two lonely travellers were pursued by a human figure, gigantic in stature, whose eyes glowed wickedly in the darkness, and who looked at the stars as if he would have dragged them from their spheres and brought them down. This mysterious man was many miles behind the objects of his pursuit; yet, although he had travelled forty miles already, he toiled on with wonderful energy and speed, and was fast gaining upon the two frail creatures labouring so painfully before him.

Will they reach the friendly shelter of the city before their enemy can overtake them?

Only Heaven can tell. The contest, apparently doubtful, seems one of death and life. We know, however, that the race is not always to the swift, nor the battle to the strong, and that beings of puny stature and little power have sometimes beaten the giants of the world.

The beneficent angel throbbed in heaven, stretched forth her hands towards the weary women, and

seemed as if she would draw them onward and shield
them from the impending evil.

CHAPTER XIV.

A DREAM AND A FACT.

THE sleep of Pate Fox was more than restless on
Saturday night and Sunday morning. It was disturbed and strangled by terrible and fantastic dreams.
For these phenomena two causes might be as-
signed. Pate had met some of the reddest of the
Radicals late in the evening, and from the colour of
their talk he could easily perceive that something
desperate was in the wind. It was little wonder,
therefore, that he occasionally started in his sleep,
as if dazzled by the flash of Radical pikes in collision
with the swords of King George's troops.

But his mind was also busy with the mission
with which he and Bob Lintie had been intrusted;
and all sorts of figures in the strangest costumes—
gipsies, soldiers, and wigged judges — arose and
passed through the theatre of his dreams.

At length Pate dreamed that he was pursued by
some enemy whose face he could not see. He was
about to be slaughtered, as he thought, when a young

veiled maiden put a sword quickly into his hand.
With this weapon the twister turned upon his foe,
and was in the act of lifting his hand to strike him
dead, when he awoke.

For a minute Pate thought that he must still be
dreaming, because he felt that he still grasped in his
hand the hilt of the sword which the maiden had
given him. He was afraid to look at his hand, lest
the weapon might vanish, like so many other dream-
treasures of his past life. Mustering courage, however, he withdrew his eyes from the ceiling, whereon
he had fixed them, and looked at his right hand to
see what he was clutching so firmly. Pate laughed,
but not outrageously, when he saw what was in his
hand. Instead of the sword of his dream, he grasped
a copy of the New Testament, which Christine Dundas had given him as a present, and which, in his
dream, he had picked up from a small table standing near the head of his bed. Pate lay and mused,
still holding the sacred volume in his hand.

'It's a queer dream—by ordinar' queer—that a
peacefu' man like me should dream o' fechtin' wi' a
sword, and wauken wi' the Testament in my haun'!
After a', it's maybe the best sword that a man can
fecht wi'. It beats a' carnal weapons. The Almichty used to speak to His prophets in dreams. I
wonner—na, I'm no a prophet, and it canna be that
He—yet naething's impossible wi' Him. Maybe the

dream was sent as a warning. My mither was a
steeve believer in dreams, and she could aye pick
a meaning out o' them. The sword in my dream
was gi'en me by a veiled leddy, and, if there's angels
on earth, this best o' books was gi'en me by ane o'
them. Could an angel frae Heeven gie me onything
better? It's no possible, for it cam frae Heeven, at
onyrate. It *cam!* Is't no aye coming yet? It's
surely no to be thought that God wad stop sending
His Word. Sae lang, at least, as man'll no tak' it,
it may be said that He aye sends't; and to the man
wha opens his heart to it for the first time it is just
as if Christ had spoken for the first time in this
world, and revealed the wonderfu' mercy o' His
Faither in Heeven. The name o' God is an auld
name, but His mercy is new every day. It's a bonnie
bit bookie,' and Pate patted and stroked the New
Testament given to him by Christine Dundas as if it
had been a living child. ' It brings me in mind o'
auld times, when my sister and me used to sit at
our mither's knee, after our faither was taen to his
lang hame, and she read to us out o' a wee Testament like this the true words o' the true life.' Then,
after a reflective pause, he continued : ' She wad hae
ca'd my dream a real warning, and maybe it is.
How did the book come into my haun' and me soun'
sleeping? Could I tak' it up mysel'? or was't put
there by some ither body? But wha could it be?

They say that sometimes, for guid ends, the angels
and the spirits are allowed to walk the earth. I
dinna ken what to think o't, but mony that are baith
guid and clever believe't; and I can gang sae far as
to believe mysel' that naething guid is impossible to
our Maker and our Saviour. Gudesake, if onybody
heard me the now they wad think I was a Christian,
when I'm far frae that. *To ken* and *to be* are no
just the same thing in godly affairs. I can see weel
eneugh what I ought to be; but how to be it? Ay,
ay, that's it—that's what troubles me. "The difference atween *ken* and *can*," as Lewis Dundas says,
"is something awfu'. Every fule can wish; but it
takes a wise man to will." I doubt I'm a useless
pickle o' banes—runkled in soul and body—a pile o'
caff, blawn to and fro by the thochtless winds.'

At this moment the hour of six was struck from
a distant steeple, which made Pate leap from his bed
with an amount of agility which somewhat belied his
previous self-depreciation.

'I maun be up and aff,' he said; 'it's time that
Bob and me were awa to see if we can meet thae puir
women, and save them, if possible, frae their enemies, whaever they may be. The deevil tak' them;
if I had my thoom in their thrapples, they wadna do
muckle mair wrang either to man or woman on this
earth.'

While thus speaking, Pate was trying to put on

his clothes, but somehow without much success. Several times he stopped and asked himself what was the matter. For a time, however, he could not fathom his apparent stupidity. He sat down to think it over, when, putting his right hand on his knee, he discovered that he still clutched the New Testament, which had hampered him so much from getting into his ' sair-mended duddies,' as he called his trousers. He smiled a curious smile when he saw the cause of his discomfiture, and said, addressing himself,

' O'd, Pate, but ye're wiser than ye thocht. If ye had aye keepit a haud o' the Scriptures as ticht as that, ye wad hae been a different man the day, breeks or nae breeks. There's surely something gaun to happen. If it wasna that ye were to meet Bob Lintie, ye should step up to St. John's and hear your freen Dr. Chalmers, the only prophet o' God in this sinfu' city. And ye may ca' me a leear,'if ye wadna get something frae him that wad licht up the darkness o' your benichtit soul. Try and gang up.'

Pate then wriggled himself into his clothes, washed his face, made himself as decent as the appliances of his toilet table could afford, breakfasted, and went forth to find his friend Bob, in order that they might go upon their singular and apparently hopeless quest.

The morning was beautiful. The sun had been

early up, but the larks had been up before him, and
had sprinkled the world with the melodious dew of
their psalms.   There is something inexpressibly fine
in the calm of a clear bright April Sabbath morning.
In the country everything wears an aspect of poetic
beauty and spiritual holiness, in which there is no
element of austerity.   At that season the earth is in
the hopeful mood.   All things are growing from less
to more—springing and expanding, flushing into new
colours, and becoming lovelier in form; the air purer
and sweeter; the fields, woods, and hills more fasci-
nating to the eye and attractive to the fancy and
imagination; and the sky, with its sea-like spaces of
ineffable blue, crossed and recrossed with all manner
of fine fantasticalities of cloud, is itself a region of
divinest marvels.   Interfuse all this with every kind
of music, from the almost visible twinkle of the
wren's voice, deep in a green dingle, to the rounder
and more persistent melodies of the mavis and the
blackbird, and up to the holy and passionate lyric-
ripple of the lark—and the earth on a Sabbath morning will seem to the sympathetic and intelligent soul
a dwelling-place as fit for the immortals as for mortal
men and women.

But even in the city there are signs of spring.
The cages of the bird-fanciers, so long silent, now
become vocal.   Three or four stories up, sometimes
five or six, you will, if you have good eyes, perceive

here and there, hung outside some tailor's or cobbler's
window, a cage containing a favourite bird—gold-
finch, canary, linnet, lark, blackbird, or mavis. These
creatures, although far from their native woods and
secret haunts, and hemmed in by the sternest phenomena of human civilisation, still feel the inherent
instincts which governed them in a state of freedom.
They know when the spring is approaching, and
begin to exhibit the restlessness of musical and pair-
ing inspiration. Nothing delights them so much as
being placed outside in the sunshine, which seems
to bring to their seething imaginations visions of
leafy palaces among the woodland greenery, hidden
wooings in the airy-swinging branches, and the co-
operative virtues of nest-building, with all its sequent
raptures. Passing beneath one of these cages, you
will hear a clear well-known voice far above, and
suddenly stop, vaguely dreaming that you cannot be
in the city, but in a forest, or among the fields. A
glance upwards reveals the reality, and you pass on,
drenched with the music, and blessing the small
heroic throat. Even the fussy chattering sparrow,
the democrat and stump orator of birds, is a sort of
spring prophet in his way, and does not altogether
fail to convey to the pent-up denizens of city lanes
some faint knowledge of the great and beautiful
changes which have come over the face of Nature.

As Pate and Bob walked along, making short cuts

through by-streets, and discussing what they would do, they could not help talking about the fineness of the morning, and listening, with a kind of half-humorous glee, to the happy bird-voices that occasionally assailed their ears from house-tops, and from suspended cages.

By a series of windings, the pair emerged suddenly upon the High-street; and on turning the corner of Duke-street, they saw a crowd of people, who appeared to be curiously excited.

'What's that, Bob?' asked Pate.

'Gude kens. The folk are reading a big bill on the wa'.'

'It's the Radicals, I'll wager a groat. I was sure frae my dreams that something was gaun to happen. Is that Andrew Hardie among the crowd?'

'I think it is,' replied Bob. 'Come, and he'll tell us what it's a' about.'

The two went forward to the crowd, and edged themselves near to Hardie, who was apparently scanning the placard.

'I say, Hardie,' said Pate, touching the young Radical with his elbow, 'what's up this morning?'

'In gude time, my Lord Twister,' answered Hardie, in mild derision. 'Hae you and your aristocratic freens got your mansions and castles put in order? Answer me that first.'

'We're a' gay weel, general, and are likely to be

sae for a wheen years to come yet. As for mysel,
I'm no sae badly aff for arms. I hae a poker, a pair
o' tangs, the butt-end o' a fishing-rod, and twa-three
legs o' a broken chair. I expect that wi' thae, I'll
be able to keep out a' the Rads that are likely to
fash me. For provision, I hae a half-peck o' oat-
meal, a laaf, three red herring, a quarter o' saut but-
ter, and a chappin o' sour douk; and I consider
mysel safe eneuch wi' that for the langest o' the
Radical campaigns. Hae ye got ony o' your forces
in the field yet?'

'Ye'll no cry that at the Cross. But, Pate, I
wad advise ye to tak' in the slack o' your tongue, or
ye'll be made to jeer on the wrang side o' your mouth
some o' thae days. Read that address there, and
tremble!'

'I canna get near eneuch, Andrew,' Pate replied
in a low voice;—and we may add that all the foregoing serio-comic banter was conducted in a safe key.
'But I may say,' continued the twister, 'that if it's
some Radical nonsense, as I jalouse it is, I'm no the
least fear't for't, ony mair than for a puff o' pease-
meal. It'll blaw owre, like the win' that blew owre
Campsie Fells, and didna kill a midden cock. Let
me warn ye, though, Andrew, my man, that unless
Alexander the Great's ghost has come frae Greece or
heeven to command your forces, there's nae hope
for ye.'

'I hear ye, Pate; but as ye're neither a prophet nor the son o' a prophet, your words are no inspired.'

'It doesna need a prophet to declare that it's no in the power o' twa-three ill-fed, ill-cled, and ill-led Radical weavers, spinners, coopers, cobblers, and sic-like trasherie to overthrow, knock down, and tramp out a great Government like ours. A' ye'll be able to do, Hardie, will be to get some o' yoursels banished or hanged. Tak' my advice, and for your mither's sake, if no for God's or your ain, leave a' this folly to the fules that bred it in the cat-wutted chaumers o' their brains.'

'Thank ye for naething, Pate. Ye're ane o' them that widna gie ae drap o' their bluid to save their sinking country. Ye'll no figure in the Book o' Martyrs, or I'm cheated.'

'Ye'll no be cheated, Andrew; for I dinna expect to figure in that tearfu' book. I'll keep my bluid till it's wanted, and then—'

'Weel, and what then?'

'I'll no pour't into a sheuch, as some o' ye are likely to do if ye come within a mile o' King Geordie's sogers. Wha's yon?'

This question referred to an important-looking personage who was approaching from the region of George-street, and who seemed eager, like other people, to know what the crowd were about. Bob Lintie answered Pate's question by remarking,

'That's your namesake, Andrew—that's Jamie Hardie, the Justice o' the Peace.'

'Are ye sure, Bob?'

'As sure's ye're Pate Fox.'

'Then, Andrew,' said Pate earnestly, 'ye'd better tak' care o' what ye say. Namesakes are no freens.'

'I dinna care a preen-pint for the hale bench o' justices,' answered Hardie, as he pressed forward to take his turn at reading the address, which began thus:

'*To the Inhabitants of Great Britain and Ireland.*

'Friends and Countrymen,—Roused from that torpid state in which we have been sunk for many years, we are at length compelled, from the extremity of our sufferings, and the contempt heaped upon our petitions for redress, to assert our rights at the hazard of our lives, and proclaim to the world the real motives which have induced us to take up arms for the redress of our common grievances.'

The address then went on to say that 'the interests of all classes are the same; that the protection of the life and property of the rich man is the interest of the poor man, and, in return, it is the interest of the rich to protect the poor from the iron grasp of despotism.

'Our principles are few, and are founded on the

basis of our constitution, which was purchased with
the dearest blood of our ancestors, and which we
swear to transmit to posterity unsullied, or perish in
the attempt. Equality of rights, not of property, is
the object for which we contend, and which we
consider as the only security for our liberties and
lives. . . .

' "Liberty or death!" is our motto, and we have
sworn to *return home* in triumph, or return no
more!'

The address then endeavoured to enlist the sym-
pathies of the army, and everybody in general was
called upon to come forward and assist in replacing
to Britons ' those rights consecrated to them by
Magna Charta and the Bill of Rights, and sweep
from our shores that corruption which has degraded
us below the dignity of men.'

' All public and private property' was declared to
be inviolable. Then,

' During the continuance of so momentous a
struggle, we earnestly request of all to desist from
their labour from and after this day, the 1st of April,
and attend wholly to the recovery of their rights;
and consider it as the duty of every man not to re-
commence until he is in possession of those rights,
which distinguish the freeman from the slave, viz.
that of giving consent to the laws by which he is
governed.'

Persons found carrying arms against the regenerators of their country were to be considered as
traitors, and treated accordingly.

'By order of the Committee of Organisation for
forming a Provisional Government.

'*Glasgow*, April 1, 1820.'

While Andrew Hardie, the Radical, was engaged
reading this startling document, James Hardie, the
Justice, approached. Glancing eagerly at the placard, he seemed to grasp the full meaning of it without reading a dozen lines, and he at once shouted,
in a loud voice,

'You men there, I call upon you, in the King's
name, to stop reading that treasonable address, and
go peaceably to your homes.'

The crowd became still more excited, and some
who were frightened at the sound of the authorita-
tive voice, took themselves quietly away. Pate and
Bob retired to the middle of the street, where they
stood watching; but Radical Hardie stood his ground,
and refused either to move or stop reading the address. The Justice, wroth at his obstinacy, cried
fiercely,

'You, fellow, cease at once reading that vile
trash, and tear it from the wall.'

'D'ye mean me?' asked Hardie, turning round
and staring at the Justice.

'Yes, I mean you, and I command you to destroy that treasonable bill!'

'*You* command *me!* Fellow, I decline to obey. I've been commanded by a better man than ever ye hae been, or ever will be, an' I dinna gie that for your command!' and Hardie snapped his fingers in the Justice's face. 'Ye can tear't doun yoursel after I read it.'

Justice Hardie now became thoroughly enraged, and rushed forward to tear the placard from the wall; but the young Radical hustled him aside, saying,

'After I'm done, if ye please.'

'You will answer to your country for this, you young scoundrel!' said the Justice, foaming.

'It'll be mair easy for me to answer to my country for that, ye kirk saunt, than it'll be for you to answer to God for—'

The rest of the sentence was hissed into the ear of the Justice, who from the bursting purple of anger became suddenly white as a sheet with surprise and something very like terror. All that he could do, or all he cared to do, was to glare wildly at Hardie, and shake his fist ominously as he retired, beaten in the contest which he had needlessly provoked.

'He'll no forget that in a hurry,' said Hardie, addressing Pate and Bob, in passing.

'Ye may be sure o' that, Andrew, whatever it

was that made him sae like a ghost. But I wad
advise ye,' added Pate, ' to keep out o' his road. I
could see murder in his e'e. Tak' my advice, and
gie him a wide berth.'

' He can try his warst.'

' There's treason in that bill,' said Bob Lintie
seriously; ' think, Andrew, what the warst o' that
may be.'

' I ken brawly that he wadna stick at bringing a
man to the gallows; but I'll no stick at duty for a'
that, an' the warst may come if it likes. The best
will maybe come next.'

CHAPTER XV.

A STRANGE MEETING.

WEARILY, wearily, wearily, on that beautiful Sabbath morning, two worn and woeful women approached Glasgow from the east. They had travelled all night, and at dawn of day had stopped for
half an hour at the village of Condorret, a few miles
from the city.

This fortunate rest was due to the kindliness of
John Baird, a young man whom they saw in a little
garden, reading a piece of printed paper. As the
women approached, Baird hid the document quickly

away in his pocket, and after interchanging a few
words with the travellers, led them into his father's
house, where, early as it was, they were speedily
supplied with the means of refreshment.

Seeing how fatigued they were, the pitiful house-
mother pressed them to remain. But the mere idea
of lingering seemed to make them more eager to
continue their journey. They started, and looked
wildly about, as if afraid of being detained. Resist-
ing, with thanks, the temptation to stay, they pushed
once more towards the city—slowly, slowly, painfully, and wearily, and with many a backward glance
of mingled suspicion and fear.

Nor were their suspicions and fears unfounded.
Far behind them came a tall and powerful man, who
was evidently in pursuit of somebody. Unpausing
and unwearied, and ever keeping his eyes fixed on
the farthest reach of the road before him, this man
passed through space with extraordinary speed. From
the commencement of the pursuit till Sunday morning, he seemed sanguine of capturing the runaways.
But a few miles east of Condorret, as day began to
dawn, he stopped suddenly, his face clouded with
anger and chagrin. Swearing a horrible oath about
being baffled by two women, he struck off the main
road away to the south, muttering as he went that it
would be better to let Sir John know at once of their
escape.

After some hours of hard walking, he reached the Hermitage, but only in time to learn that Sir John had just gone to Glasgow. But where to find him there? In St. John's Church, where Dr. Chalmers was that day to preach some special sermon. The man at once took the road to Glasgow, but not without being carefully scanned by two men who happened to be lounging near the Hermitage, and who, with the aid of a swift horse and a gig, contrived to reach the city before the traveller, so as to be able to watch his manœuvres.

Meanwhile, the two travelworn women approached the city as the church bells began to ring. The sound seemed to cheer them. There was something in the music of the bells, as it vibrated through the still clear Sabbath air, which gave them a sense of protection. The burden of apprehension which had so long weighed upon and crushed their spirits was growing lighter, and hope, though still very faintly and chaotically, began to dawn upon them.

'This is Glasgow, now, Swallow, is it?'

'Yes, Nightingale, this is the city, thank gudeness for it! We couldna gang a mile mair. But whaur'll we seek a lodging for the night? It might hae been better if we had gane to Hamilton.'

'Do not fear, Nelly—shall I call you Nelly, now that we have got away from Hawk?'

Nightingale shivered as she spoke, while a wan-

dering gleam broke in her eyes like the lighting of a
lamp veiled with gauze. Swallow, now called Nelly,
looked at her mistress with alarm, caught her hand
softly, and said,

' Ay, ay, ca' me Nelly, ca' me Nelly, and I'll ca'
ye my leddy, and we'll trust in God, and He'll gang
wi' us, as He's done before, and maybe we'll meet
wi' them that'll be kinder to us—auld freens, ye ken
—d'ye hear, my leddy ?'

It seemed doubtful whether Nightingale had heard
Nelly at all, for she looked absent and inattentive,
either wholly absorbed with some despotic idea, or
entirely vacant. Nelly whispered something in her
ear, which had the intended effect of dispersing the
mists that enveloped her mind.

' Yes, yes,' she said eagerly, ' I remember. Do
you think we shall see them soon ?' and then, paus-
ing, ' Shall we see them at all ? O Nelly, it is so
old a dream—so old, so far away, and so painful—
so painful !'

' Come, my leddy, come ; there's twa men watching us—come quick !'

' O God, Nelly, it is not Hawk ?'

' No, no ; but come awa.'

' Where shall we go ?' Nightingale asked wearily,
letting herself be led away like a child.

The two women were walking westward along the
Gallowgate at this time, and when they arrived at

the corner of East Campbell-street, Nelly paused for
a moment considering; but seeing crowds of well-
dressed people going up that street, she suddenly
mingled with them, and drifted with the current,
hoping by that means to escape the notice of the
men whom she had seen looking at them. As these
two men followed the travellers closely, one of them
said hurriedly,

'Look at them again, Bob. D'ye no think they hae
the appearance o' twa that hae been on the tramp?'

'There can be nae doubt o' that, Pate; but how
mony puir folk are on the tramp every day?'

'Ne'er fash your heid wi' that. Let us follow,
and watch whaur they gang.'

They were not long held in suspense, for as Nelly
and her mistress approached the upper end of the
street, the latter, seeing the people streaming into
St. John's Church, was seized with a sudden fancy
to enter also, and could not be persuaded against the
idea.

'You must follow me, Nelly,' said Nightingale
swiftly, and with unwonted energy; 'it is long since
we worshipped God inside a church. We must do
it now, for now is the time—the accepted time.
Come away! Do you not remember,' she continued,
kindling, 'how often we were told that all good
comes with prayer and worship? Don't be afraid,
Nelly; keep close to me, come—come—come!'

Thus speaking, Nightingale all but dragged her companion into the church. Pate and Bob approached as they entered, and the latter remarked,

' I doubt we're wrang, Pate.'

' It's possible. But I wad like to see mair o' them. What d'ye think we should do? Wad it no be a guid thing to gang in and hear the doctor? There's to be some great sermon the day.'

' The doctor's aye great. Wait till we see wha's coach this is coming up.'

In half a minute the carriage to which Bob referred stopped at the church door.

' It's Lord Carmyle,' said Pate. And sure enough his lordship stepped from the carriage, and was about to enter the church, when he got his eye on Pate, stopped, and motioned him to approach.

' Well, Pate, any report?'

' No muckle, my lord. We hae seen twa women that we thocht micht be them Campbell spoke o'.'

' And where are they?'

' They've just gane into the kirk.'

Lord Carmyle shook his head, indicating doubt. of their identity. Then, after a moment's reflection, he said,

'But you might do worse, Pate, than go in and hear a good sermon, and afterwards you could perhaps keep your eye on the two.'

Pate nodded in assent, and his lordship entered

the church, followed immediately by the two companions, who contrived to get an inch of seat a-piece
in the eastern side-aisle near the door.

It is not demanded by the necessities of this tale,
or we could enrich it with the portrait of one of the
most remarkable men of his time. But Dr. Chalmers
is sufficiently well known. In 1820 he was in the
vigour of life, and had reached the splendour of his
fame as a preacher. The immense popularity which
he had won in connection with the Tron Kirk, after
his settlement in Glasgow, was fully maintained in
his new church of St. John's, to which he was presented by the Town Council. When he preached, it
was not to a local congregation, but one drawn from
all parts of the city and country round about. Of
the great orator's eloquence, it will serve our present
purpose to say that its leading characteristic was
irresistible and overwhelming power. It shook and
shattered the egotisms and meannesses of men as
by flashes of lightning and shocks of thunder. The
little devils of vanity, pride, selfishness, envy, jeal-
ousy, spite, revenge, and their infinite kindred of
raven-wings, which curse mankind, could not withstand the consuming splendour of this man's eloquence. By its fiery scourge, he sent them packing
back to the hell of their birth—at least for a time,
and in many cases for ever.

On this particular Sunday morning the sermon

was one of great power. Part of that power arose
from a singular under-current of pathos which ran
through it, and which made the listeners feel as if,
between the pauses of the tempestuous eloquence,
they heard the sighing of a woman or the sobbing of
a child. Consequently, the sermon was one which
not only shook and pierced, but softened and melted.

There was not a single person present untouched
by the preacher's burning and penetrating words.
But two persons seemed more conspicuously affected.
These were Sir John Home and the poor way-worn
Nightingale. Sir John was shaken and pierced, but
neither softened nor melted. In the intense light
flashed out by the orator the Baronet felt that one
of two things must be true—either that he himself
must be a scoundrel, or the preacher a liar. He
knew which view was correct, but he was only shaken
with prophetic terror, not tortured by remorse or
softened by the spirit of repentance.

It was upon poor Nightingale that the overwhelming force of the sermon happily fell. She was
at first stunned, blinded, and utterly confounded.
It was like the voice of an archangel she heard, and
she had some notion that she must be sitting in
front of the judgment-seat. Afterwards, however,
as the preacher advanced from sentence to sentence,
the whirling chaos of her mind gradually vanished,
and her thoughts assumed a clearness and an order

which they had not known for years. She was shaken, pierced, softened, melted, and lifted up as upon wings, and under the spell of that wonderful voice she seemed to unlive all the mental confusion of her past life.

When the voice of the preacher ceased, Nightingale rose in her seat, impelled by an irrepressible impulse. In rising, her gaze became riveted on the family seat of Dr. Chalmers, where Lord Carmyle sat. At the same instant his lordship caught sight of the rising figure, and the eyes of the two were at once fixed on each other. Both seemed spell-bound. A beam of golden light fell upon the form of Nightingale, who stood pale and trembling, but strangely transformed in the sacred radiance, looking younger by many years than she actually was.

A cry of mingled joy and distress seemed to escape the lips of Nightingale and Lord Carmyle at the same moment, and they made as if they would rush into each other's arms.

Sir John Home occupied a pew on the opposite side of the church from that on which Lord Carmyle sat. Just when the sermon was finished, Sir John heard a slight movement behind him, and then somebody touched him lightly on the shoulder. On turning quietly round to see what was the matter, he exclaimed, in a scared whisper,

' Good God, Hawk, what are you doing here ?'

'They have both escaped,' Hawk answered significantly.

The Baronet grew livid, and muttered a string of language which, had it been audible, would have brought down upon him the thunders of the Church. But upon Hawk, who was keenly scanning the congregation, the words produced no effect whatever. Sir John then asked whether he had any knowledge of the whereabouts of the runaways. Hawk did not reply for a moment, but kept his attention fixed on a particular seat in the church. Pate Fox and Bob Lintie were engaged watching the same spot. When Sir John repeated his question almost savagely, Hawk only pointed with his finger to the region upon which he had glued his own eyes. Following the cunning hint, Sir John's eye at length lighted upon a spectacle which froze the blood in his heart. It was at the very moment that Nightingale, standing up from her seat, suffused by the mellow beam of sunlight, had fixed her gaze upon Lord Carmyle, as he upon her. The confederates heard the mutual exclamation of the two, and shuddered as they heard it. Sir John sat helpless; and Hawk stood immovable as a statue of stone. They could only watch the singular drama going on before their eyes.

When Nightingale uttered her pathetic cry of recognition, she moved hurriedly from her seat, in spite of Swallow's confused attempts to prevent her.

Having got clear of her companion, she rushed with
outstretched arms towards Lord Carmyle, while he,
equally excited and astonished, rushed towards her,
and caught her in his arms as she was about to fall,
crying faintly, ' O, James ! O, James !'

'Almighty God !' he gasped, 'is this indeed
Margaret ? My own Margaret ! my love, my love !
O, my dear, do not die again, after so many years
of death !'

Lord Carmyle became ghastly and faint, and
probably his newly-recovered treasure would have
dropped from his grasp, had not a gentleman sitting
near caught her helpless form, while supporting his
lordship at the same time. They were both at once
removed to the seclusion of the vestry.

'Sir John,' whispered Hawk, 'the game is up.
We had better both of us put the seas between us
and Scotland.'

'Not yet, Hawk. Don't you see Swallow sitting
confounded yonder ? Secure her at all hazards ;
keep her in the city till dark ; and then bring her to
the Hermitage. Quick !'

Hawk disappeared like a shot, and unfortunately
succeeded in the design suggested by Sir John. It
only, however, retarded their fate for a few days.

Then, of course, instead of going to the aid of
his cousin, the Baronet thought it more prudent to
drive home at once. But he was driven to the Her-

mitage by other creatures than common steeds. The
Furies leashed themselves to his soul, and whirled
it through endless hells of agony and terror. He
felt that God's curse had fallen upon and demolished
the empire of hope which he had built upon a foun-
dation of most inhuman wrong. Nor was it less
impressive and appalling that the blow was dealt in
God's own house. It seemed as if the prophet who
had been thundering the divine oracles from the
pulpit had brought down the long-slumbering vengeance of the Almighty.

The foregoing scene, occurring at the end of the
sermon, when there is sometimes a long pause, was
enacted so quickly, that it hardly interrupted the
concluding services for a single minute. But those
who were near enough to see the incident were more
than surprised; many pious worshippers were scan-
dalised at what seemed so very little different from
a love-scene in a theatre. When they came to know
the facts of the case, they were thrilled with pity,
and awe-struck at the evidently providential character of the meeting. It was only God, they believed,
who rules and overrules, who could bring about such
wonders.

'Weel, Pate,' said Bob, when the pair had got
into the street with the stream of worshippers,
'what d'ye think o' that? It beats onything ever I
saw in a kirk.'

'D'ye mean the sermon, or the—'

'I dinna mean the sermon; I mean the—what can we ca't? It looked sae queer at first; yet it was sae pitifu' and serious.'

'Ye may say that, Bob. I never saw a man sae like death as Lord Carmyle was when he catched the woman in his arms. She was like a ghost hersel'.'

'And what a fearfu' cry they baith gied when they saw each ither for the first time! It made my very bluid cauld.'

'I wonner, Pate, wha she can be?'

'There's a mystery in't;' and the twister shook his head weightily as he spoke, and looked as if he could say a thing or two on the subject, but chose for some unfathomable reason to hold his tongue in the mean time.

The two cronies had, however, bungled their work somewhat. They had been so absorbed with the scene between Lord Carmyle and Nightingale that they lost sight of Swallow altogether. In the slight commotion produced by the greater scene, Hawk was enabled to spirit her away by using a gipsy threat, which never failed to terrify the poor creature into passive and despairing obedience.

CHAPTER XVI.

TERROR AND ERROR.

HAD a bolt fallen from heaven and demolished the Tontine, or had the cholera assumed bodily form, and stalked through the streets, it could not have produced more excitement among all classes in Glasgow than did the Radical address which, from every wall, glared and flamed upon the citizens on Sunday morning.

The weaker-kneed people expected the ground to open and swallow them; and even the strongest and most sensible, in spite of their strength and sense, were haunted by fears of the deadliest quality and shape.

Clergymen prayed against the impending revolution, and the possible massacre. Manufacturers and merchants trembled in all their pockets; and the tills of the grocers and the safes of the bankers were guarded with the most tender affection. Credit drew in her sensitive horns, and for many days lay as quiescent as a blind snail that has been touched by some other crawling spirit.

All Sunday, crowds of artisans met at corners, or walked up and down the streets discussing the Radical proclamation. The excitement was universal and intense, and it deepened every hour and each succeeding day. What would occur was a mystery; but in the general apprehension the air seemed loaded with mortal events, which might burst in or over the city at any moment.

Captain Batwing was busier than ever, and so were the authorities, upon whom the cunning Captain poured daily a stream of information, partly gathered by himself, but mostly by his sleepless corps of night-birds.

On Sunday evening, the question which lashed the magisterial and mercantile mind was whether the people would obey the summons addressed to them by the Radical Committee, strike work, and not return to their looms, benches, anvils, and hammers, until their political rights were conceded.

On Monday morning the question was solved. The people leaped from bed at an early hour, but, with few exceptions, they did not return to their work. For nearly a week, factories and loomshops were empty, shuttles were silent, and webs remained unwoven.

But the Three Weird Sisters of Fate, invisible to the common eye, were secretly spinning Three Threads of Destiny—one Thread apiece for Three Doomed Men.

When the magistrates saw definitely the temper of the people, they prepared energetically for the worst. They issued several proclamations, which, however, did nothing to soothe the popular mind, or calm the rising tempest.

One of the documents declared that 'the whole military power of the district will be employed in the most decisive manner to prevent the laws of the land being insulted and violated by an audacious display of numbers by the disloyal;' and that the 'consequences will be fatal to all who venture to oppose and resist the overwhelming power at our disposal.'

The overwhelming power thus alluded to amounted in a few days to nearly 5000 troops, who failed, however, to frighten the people back to their looms, benches, and forges. The East Lothian and Ayr Yeomanry were a beautiful sight to see as they pranced hither and thither about the city, their clear buttons burning, and their maiden swords flashing, in the sun. Not less formidable and magnificent was the Regiment of Glasgow Sharpshooters. This corps consisted of gentlemen picked from the leading families of the city; and from all accounts it must have been one of the best-appointed troops that Glasgow has ever produced. One of its most conspicuous members was its colonel, Samuel Hunter, then editor of the *Glasgow Herald*. Portly as Sir John Falstaff, and hardly less witty, he was everywhere welcome and at all times a favourite. His presence, like that of the sun, communicated light and cheerfulness; and amid his special companions and friends, he was the reigning Jupiter, always ready with a bolt of wit or a genial beam of humour.

These gallant corps would have been capable of great things, backed as they were by a large body of regular troops. Had need been, they would have galloped through a wall of enemies in slashing style. Happily that need never arose, so that their services were confined to the negative function of prevention. All that can be said for them, therefore, is that they probably saved the city from the horrors of riot or insurrection.

But they could not turn into smiles the scowls that were upon the face of the populace; nor could the troops, 5000 though they were, prevent the Radicals from putting forth all their energies in perfecting their schemes. Night and day, but especially at night, secret meetings continued to be held, and secret couriers were sent throughout all Radicaldom to prepare the patriots for the blow that was about to be struck. It was proclaimed everywhere that England had already leapt to arms, or was about to leap; and all that was now wanted was that Scotland should follow her example, shoulder muskets, pick up pike and pistol, and strike for liberty.

Mr. Dundas was seriously anxious about Alan, not altogether for Christine's sake, but as much for the young fellow's own sake. He knew that a lover's quarrel was a thing more easily healed than a trea-

sonable quarrel with the Government, and he determined to make another effort to prevent Alan from
plunging into the Radical gulf now yawning for its
victims.

Dr. Bannatyne, whom Mr. Dundas first consulted
on the subject, could tell him nothing about Alan,
except that since Saturday he had looked unnaturally
glum and grim, ' as if he had quarrelled with his
sweetheart, or was about to commit murder.'

' That's a good shot, Doctor.'

' I don't quite comprehend ?'

' There has actually been a lovers' quarrel; and
it is as probable as not that Alan will help to commit
some Radical folly which, in being treason, may also
be slaughter, and therefore not unlike murder.'

' Curse their stupidity and rascality!' roared the
Doctor. ' I wish I had the purging of them. I
should give them a pill that would sicken them
against universal suffrage, annual Parliaments, and
the ballot for a month to come. But I do wonder at
Alan. Yet why should I wonder? He had the misfortune to be born under a romantic star; and what
is worse, he had you, Lewis, for his first political
schoolmaster—a pernicious position for a soul so
sanguine and poetic.'

' Thank you, Doctor. But I need hardly tell you
that he never learnt from me anything about the
poetry of pikes.'

'Probably not. It would be sufficient if you taught him something about the poetry of principles. Pikes are the logical sequences of certain principles. Your philosophical Radicalism is a sort of poetic treason. You can hardly blame an honest youth for carrying his principles into the practicalities of hard steel. But, seriously, does that idiotic address really mean anything?'

'It means mischief—and immediately.'

'But why don't the magistrates prevent it? There are as many troops in the city as might eat the Radicals, and their pikes to boot. Prevention is better than cure.'

'If all diseases were prevented, doctors — political, magisterial, and medical — might shut up shop.'

'Fairly hit. Yet there ought to be limits to the vile policy of "Let-alone."'

'That's my own belief, and that's why I ask your help to cure Alan.'

'I suspect, Dundas, that you who drugged him must also undrug him. He is quite beyond my skill. To tell you the truth, however, I should like to see him saved. He is of great use to me, and I begin to believe that he will adorn his profession should nothing interfere with his studies. Hang all Radicals!'

'That is to say, hang the salt of the earth. Remember, Doctor, that Radicals and Rebels are not convertible terms.'

'They are so logically, and would be so practically, if cowardice didn't hamper philosophy. But what's the use of talking? You are as much beyond cure as Alan himself. By the way, have you heard about this most extraordinary Carmyle affair?'

'I have heard a rumour, which is far too romantic to be true.'

'It is true, nevertheless,' replied the Doctor.

'True!'

'True as truth. I have visited Lady Carmyle, his lordship's wife, who, after so many years of absence, has marvellously reappeared. It's little less than a miracle; and there is still some mystery in the case. She seems actually to have been spirited away by somebody; but who that is, has not yet been proved. And just fancy, she has been all these years travelling up and down the country with a camp of gipsies! You may well stare and look incredulous. I doubt she must have been out of her wits. She still wanders, and cries for a companion who was seen to enter St. John's with her, but who, it seems, disappeared, though unwillingly, with a man named Hawk. This person is supposed to have been the instrument in carrying out the abduction. He has certainly been her keeper, or rather her jailer. It is

the most unexpected and distressing revelation that
ever I heard or read of. Fiction cannot match it.'

' You call her " Lady Carmyle," and his lordship's " wife." Were they really married ? and was
there not a child ?'

' You are thinking about an old rumour, Lewis.
I know nothing precise about the matter, but I suspect that the marriage must have been a private one,
unsanctioned by the Church, but perfectly legal all
the same. I say I suspect this, because his lordship,
fearing the instability of her ladyship's health, has
persuaded his friend Dr. Chalmers to marry them
immediately. As to your other question, there certainly was a child, for her ladyship babbles about it
still in a rather confused manner—now as if it were
dead, and then as if it were still living.'

' Perhaps the person who accompanied her could
tell. Of Hawk I have heard something before, but
no good. Is her ladyship really ill ?'

' She is ill, but mainly from excitement and
fatigue. She'll recover, though it would be greatly
in her favour if her companion could be rescued from
the hands of the enemy. It is their interest to keep
her out of the way, for as she is the maid who disappeared along with her ladyship, she must know the
whole history of the crime. Happily, their whereabouts is known, so that they cannot escape.'

' I am glad to hear that; for, if I am not mistaken, the villain knows something about the origin of Alan.'

' O, you are founding on the mad adventure in Cadzow ?'

' Yes.'

' I fear there is not much to be expected from that. But try and see the lad to-day; and, if you can't make him wise by argument, I would advise you to break his leg. While it is mending, Radicalism will be broken to pieces, and he will then be safe.'

Mr. Dundas only shook his head, as he went away to search for Alan. He found him walking arm-in-arm in the College Green with Macpherson, his fellow-student and fellow-Radical, and consequently he found him in a condition of antagonism to all wisdom. With scant courtesy, he repelled all the politic suggestions which Mr. Dundas poured into his ear. Alan only softened when Christine's name was incidentally mentioned, but it occurred to his foolish fancy that Lewis wished to lead him away from his principles and his duty by making a decoy of his daughter. To some extent this was true, but Alan put a wrong construction upon it. On being told of Lord Carmyle's recovery of his wife, of which he had already heard, with all sorts of picturesque additions, he remarked that his lordship was in luck, hinting faintly how very friendly luck is to the rich

and the great. Declining to notice this bitter tone,
Mr. Dundas expected to surprise Alan by telling
him that there was a probability that his enemy
Hawk would soon be in the hands of justice. He
asked :

'Do you know what that may mean for you ?'

'I thought once,' said Alan, shaking his head,
'that the villain might be able to clear up a certain
mystery, but I doubt it now; and even the mystery
itself has ceased to puzzle or interest me. I am content to seek father and mother in my profession.'

'And very good parents, too, Alan ; but would it
be fair or humane to bring scandal upon even such
parents by flinging yourself into the arms of rebel-
lious Radicalism ?'

'Doing one's duty can never bring scandal upon
one's parents. Besides, you know, "it is the glory
of truth to be persecuted as a rebel and a heretic."
That's one of your own apothegms.'

So it was; and Mr. Dundas felt that Alan must
be left alone in the current of events, to work out for
himself the problems of the time and of his life as
he best might. He was past persuasion. But he
was not past feeling. He was bitterly miserable ;
and more than once since his quarrel with Christine
was he impelled to rush to her, confess his sins on
her breast, and cease for ever to be a Radical. Unfortunately, he was not so passionate a lover as Romeo.

He could not ascend to the height, or descend to the depth, of denying his strong, important, independent self. So he stumbled onward to the end, which was nearer than he expected.

There were five thousand troops in Glasgow; but there were secret Radical meetings that night in the city in spite of that huge military fact. There were even some drillings in certain odd corners. Captain Batwing's lieutenants attended those meetings and drillings, and at midnight they met the Captain in his den.

'Good-night, gentlemen. How goes the plot? Has it received a shock, or is it to proceed?'

'Proceed is the word, Captain,' answered King; 'there is no flinching. The proclamations of the authorities are despised, and they have been spit upon, torn down in some places, and trampled in the mud.'

'That shows spirit, at least, if not wisdom. What is the next move to be?'

'To-morrow night,' replied Lees, 'the Radicals are to assemble and march on Carron.'

'Weather permitting, I suppose?' Captain Batwing remarked, unable to resist a sneer.

'They will meet and march,' said Turner, 'although it were to rain fire. Such, at all events, is their present temper.'

'And the meeting-place and time?'

'In the fields opposite the Cathedral,' replied
King.

'A splendid spot for a camp—romantic and commanding. So be it. If the plot is so ready, so is
the counter-plot. They may march out of the city,
but they will never march back to it. They have
sworn to "return home in triumph—or return no
more." *No more* is their doom.'

'May I venture, Captain, to ask,' said Andrew
Semple anxiously, 'whether we can depend upon
that ? Will there be no chance of their escape ?'

'Console yourself, Andrew. If your enemy, Dalziel, is one of the fools, his fate is sealed. He will
never pace the streets of Glasgow again. Now, gentlemen, only few words remain to be said. You know
your several duties. Obey the command of the Radical leaders quietly, swiftly, and energetically. Assist
the movement in everything up to the point I previ-
ously indicated ; and then—every man for himself !
Do not meet me here until—well, say Sunday evening, at eleven o'clock. That will be the safest night.
We shall then settle accounts, and part, probably for
ever. Adieu in the mean time ! Be silent and cir-
cumspect.'

Let time be anticipated by the statement of two
circumstances. When Captain Batwing met his companions in spy-craft on Sunday night, they perceived
that his jaw was bound up in a clout, and that he was

singularly lame. They also perceived that the place
of Andrew Semple was vacant.

CHAPTER XVII.

ON THE BRINK.

TUESDAY the 4th of April 1820 dawned in Glasgow with a chill and sinister gleam. Morning looked
with a watery eye from beneath a fiery eyebrow, as if
he had gone late to repose after a night of riot, which
might be renewed to-day in a new form. Something
was evidently brewing both in heaven and on earth.
There seemed to exist between them only a harmony
of discord.

These baleful and unhappy aspects of the physical
world were reflected in the moral world. Or was it
the reverse? Was it man communicating to nature
the shadow of his own misery? Can man make his
own weather? or is he made by it, and whirled round
the compass like a witless weathercock?

Lord Provost Monteith awoke with a cold shiver,
as if a ghost had passed through his chamber. He
rose and shaved himself; but the touch of the razor
was uncertain, and a drop of blood appeared on his
upper lip. He staggered from the mirror, with a

vision of slaughter staining his imagination. At
breakfast his lordship looked pale, and he spoke in
monosyllables, which seemed to be picked from some
gloomy ill-tempered dictionary. All day he was restless, anxious, and irritable; and even in conference
with the municipal magnates he failed to exhibit that
serene statesmanlike air which generally character-
ised him, particularly when silent. Fortunately, his
fellow - councillors knew the nature of his lordship's
mental distemper. His face was as a glass wherein
they read strange things, which concerned themselves
not less than they concerned him.

But the two most unhappy creatures in Glasgow
that day were Alan Dalziel and Christine Dundas.
Loving each other to distraction, they were yet separated by a gulf which seemed practically impassable.
Their misery was deepened by self-accusations. Each
now saw how easy it might have been, or ought to
have been, to avoid the quarrel which parted them.
But it is always more easy to see or feel one's errors
than to confess so as to amend them. Shame cripples
confession; pride strangles repentance; and vanity
heals the scars of remorse.

More than once during the day Alan found himself hovering in the vicinity of Christine's abode,
walking as in a dreary dream. When he awoke to
the consciousness of whither he was drifting, pride
and shame bore him away in a different direction,

while love tore his heart back to Christine. He received another note from Archer, who, besides speaking more confidently than ever about the investigation into Alan's history, made a triumphant allusion to the discovery of Lady Carmyle, which he claimed the credit of having all but predicted.

'Moreover, Alan,' Archer continued, 'I have excellent grounds for believing that I shall discover Lord Carmyle's son and heir. The lad, like his mother, has hitherto been supposed to be dead. That, I can already almost prove, is a mistake. If the clue that I hold in my hand is not outrageously fallacious, the world will have soon a bit of news that will astonish it. It will astonish even you, Alan, who have so suddenly and so unaccountably shut your heart against hope. I should say that anything is possible after Lady Carmyle's reappearance.'

The young lawyer added: 'We have fearful accounts here about the revolutionary condition of your city. Is there anything in it? or is it all a romance, invented by Rumour, that epic liar, by whom the world is so easily deluded? If there is an atom of truth in what we hear, Glasgow must be in a state of siege. We are told that the streets are lined with cannon, and that there is a park of artillery planted on each of the bridges to repel the Paisley Radicals, who, ten thousand strong, are about to attack, sack,

and burn the city. Hamilton can't hold the candle
to that. We have Reformers among us, of course;
but Radicalism, in its rank Gallowgate and Calton
type, doesn't flourish in our ducal atmosphere. Up
in Strathaven, however, under the premiership of old
Wilson, whom you once met, the weavers have long
been fiercely Radical; and if the political pot con-
tinues to boil and bubble at the present interesting
rate, you may perhaps see them one of these morn-
ings rushing over Cathkin Braes like the Goths and
the Vandals. Don't imagine that, in speaking thus,
I am lightlying the Reform cause. A Reformer is
not necessarily a Radical; and a Radical needn't be
a fool or a traitor. Do you take me? Pray, Alan,
keep under the leash that passionate political spirit
of yours. At all events, keep to logic and rhetoric,
and leave pikes and rusty muskets to those who wish
to be hanged. Enough for the present. In two days
expect something important.'

'In two days,' soliloquised Alan, tragi-comically,
'you also, my good hopeful Archer, will hear of something important—much more so than discovering a
lord's heir in a mare's nest.   There will be a sound
heard that will make some of your stiff-necked gentry
think that the political day of judgment has come,
with Justice enthroned, wielding her sword and bal-
ance. O, if Justice could descend in divine person-
ality, to weigh and smite, there might be hope for the

people—the serfs that serve and yet starve; the poor, the million-headed, the million-hearted poor, whom God alone knows, and can redeem from hunger, and poverty, and crime, and despair!'

In the afternoon Macpherson entered Alan's lodgings hastily, saying:

'Come, Alan, you are wanted; the committee are met.'

'Two minutes, Mac. I have a couple of notes to write.'

The first of these missives, addressed to Christine, was couched in vague, yet tender terms. It imported to be a temporary farewell, and concluded by expressing a faint hope that they might meet soon. 'I am called out of the city upon duty of a delicate nature,' Alan wrote; 'and if I should be indefinitely detained, I beg of you, Christine, to remember me as one repenting of any injury he may have done. Your goodness and love I shall never cease to cherish in life or in death.'

The other note was addressed to his friend Archer at Hamilton. 'You write, my dear Archer,' Alan said, 'that I have shut my heart against hope. I have cause. Think of a single fact: I have somehow—though God knows how!—quarrelled with Christine; and I have been in hell ever since. As to your investigations and prophecies, I have lost all faith in them; though I can almost sympathise with

you. There is something pathetic in your credulity,
which for a lawyer is marvellous. I need not bid you
throw down the mysterious brief which you took up
through charity to me; for I know you would only
laugh at me. You are one of those who must be de-
prived of legs, arms, and your very teeth, before you
will confess defeat. I hope I won't have to pity you.
I am heartily glad that Lord Carmyle has so wonder-
fully recovered his wife. Those who saw the scene
in the church describe it as overwhelming. They
say that Dr. Chalmers, when he came to comprehend
the nature of the occurrence, was melted to tears.
Dr. Bannatyne thinks that the wandering life of Lady
Carmyle has been in favour of her health, and that
she may yet do well, if she is not confined too much
to an in-door life. So you think that Lord Carmyle's
son is alive, and that you will be able to present the
lad to his father?   My dear Archer, I am afraid you
have been overworking your brain. Take care. Do
you remember the burning sensation you used to feel
on the top of your head after a long spell of work?
You have no right to work the intellectual machinery
in this manner. It is immoral. . . I don't quite see
the force of your remarks on Radicalism and Reform.
But politics was never your *forte;* so I can forgive
your critical spiceries. Opinions formed in ignorance are not subjects for punishment, but for pity.
We have plenty of troops in Glasgow, as you remark ;.

but that has not diminished the Radical clubs by one member, nor, I believe, has it stopped a single meeting. The cause prospers under repression, as you will soon learn. This reminds me that I am about to leave the city on a delicate, and, perhaps, a dangerous duty. Should anything occur to me, I leave in your charge a certain manuscript, which, if of any value, might be published for the benefit of Mrs. Dalziel. But, my dear friend, I leave to you something infinitely dearer—the chance of winning the affections of Christine. There is no person whom I should more willingly see blessed by her wonderful beauty and goodness. God help me! You may call me a fool, Archer—and during these two or three days I have felt like one mad—yet I am too deeply pledged to my present mission to recede, even if it were desirable. Farewell!'

The note to Christine Alan left with his landlady, with the injunction to have it delivered next morning; and he took care to post the one to Archer late that night; so that it could not possibly reach its destination before noon to-morrow.

CHAPTER XVIII.

LIBERTY *v.* WHISKY.

IT was a dark night, wet and windy. Those who owned comfortable homes remained within to enjoy them. Those who lived in hovels and garrets were at home too—with their misery. It was not a night to be abroad in, or to have only the sky for a roof. Any covering was better than none in such a night. Yet in Glasgow many people were abroad, drifting through the streets in miscellaneous directions, under the pitiless rain. The banks and other important institutions were guarded by troops, who stood or moved about like so many dripping ghosts holding phantom guns in their hands. Sometimes a passer would halt before these melancholy sentinels and stare curiously. Most people who were compelled to be out on business hurried back to the shelter of their homes, afraid even to look at the soldiery. Now and then, however, a traveller in passing would glare ominously and clench his fist, as if nothing would satisfy him so much as to test its solidity upon the impassible visages of the Dragoons.

On that dismal night the principal hotels of the city, brilliant and busy, were crammed with distinguished guests. Lord Provost Monteith, with his fellow magistrates, town-clerk, fiscal, and other civic

officials, accupied chambers in the Buck's Head, Ar-
gyll - street, for the readier and more comfortable
transaction of business during the excitement of the
time.   In the same hotel were quartered the officers
of the 7th and 10th regiments of Hussars.   Major-
general Sir Thomas Bradford, the Commander-in-
chief in Scotland, with the brilliant Sir Hussey Vivian
and the rest of his staff, had his head-quarters in the
Star Hotel, at the head of Glassford-street, where also
the Lord-Advocate (Sir William Rae) and his deputies
were established.   The Black Bull overflowed with
the officers of several regiments of Scottish yeomanry,
commanded by Lord Elcho, who afterwards became
the Earl of Wemyss.   These hotels, in consequence
of the vast influx and character of their guests, were
the great centres of attraction for the space of two
weeks.   They were guarded by sentinels, and, both
by night and by day, civil and military messengers
were perpetually coming and going.

The light that streamed from these bright in-
teriors only showed how comfortable they were, and
how dismal in contrast was the world outside, where
it rained as if it had been raining since the Deluge,
and would rain till the end of the world.   But the
rain had no effect on the military activity that was
everywhere apparent.   Bodies of troops patrolled the
principal streets of the city, from the east end to the
west end, night and day,.and in foul as in fair wea-

ther. It was a night of terrible suspense. The citizens were in a condition of expectation, tortured by the feeling that something, they knew not what, was about to happen. Ideas of fire and sword and flying bullets flickered in the minds of the timid, and made them crouch closer round their comfortable or miserable hearths, shivering to hear the rain pelting on the windows, and the solemn and solid tramp, tramp of the military going their rounds.

Many curious scenes were enacted that night among the Radicals who were summoned to arms. In the mean time, we shall only give two.

*   *   *   *   *   *

'I tell ye, Dick, ye'll no steer a fit. D'ye hear how the rain is battering on the window? It's coming down in floods.'

'Gie me my coat, I tell ye,' said Dick Flynn to his anxious spouse. 'What's a shower o' rain compared wi' the flood o' misery that's drowning the heart out o' this puir country? I'll gang out though a' the sheughs in creation were in a spate. It's no to be thought that a man like me is gaun to stay ahin when a' the country is rising like ae man to fecht for liberty. We'll hae anither Bannockburn, I'll wager a shilling!'

'Deil nor ye were drowned in Bannockburn, and liberty alang wi' ye! Hae ye no plenty o' liberty? Wha's meddling wi' ye? And what's liberty in a

night like this ? Tak' aff your claes and gang to your
bed, ye silly guse, and no mak' a fule o' baith me and
yoursel', wi' your daft Radical pliskies. Ye'll get nae
coat frae me this nicht.'

'Will I no, though ? D'ye see this ?' and Dick
whipped something from beneath the bed. 'I'll ram
this pike through ye, if ye dinna gie me out my coat
and my shoon in the wink o' a hen's e'e. D'ye hear,
Maggie, my braw woman ? Wha's maister now, I
wad like to ken ? "Now's the day, and now's the
hour !" Out wi' my coat and shoon, or, by a' that's
gude, I'll sacrifice ye to the spirit of Liberty ! I'll
play the Roman wi' ye, wha tied his sister in her sark
to a rock in the sea to pacify the offended gods. Nane
o' your Tory tricks wi' me. I'm a patriot; and I'll
fecht till there's no as muckle bluid left in my veins
as wad slocken the drouth o' a flea.'

Mrs. Maggie Flynn stood with her back to the
door, and looked at her heroic husband with a curious gleam in her eye, and a pathetic tremble on her
lip. A stranger seeing her would have fancied that
she was cowed. But nobody knew her man so well
as Maggie: She said :

'Weel, Richard, ye'll get your coat, and ye'll get
your shoon, and onything mair ye like. But wae's
me ! I never thought it wad come to this—that ye
wad threaten to stab me wi' a pike—me, that's borne
ye twa braw sons and twa dochters that micht haud

their heids up amang the best in the Calton ! That
it should come to this ! Wae's me, wae's me ! And
this is my birthday; and I hae been thinking a' day
about what the gipsy-tinkler said when she spaed my
fortune. I was a bit young thing then, and laughed
at her; but her words are come true. " Beware o'
your birthday," she said, " and tak' care o' your
man's coat and shoon. Wat feet and a wat back are
no guid for rheumatics; and rheumatics are bad for
love." She was a true prophet, though I laughed at
her. " Beware o' your birthday !" Weel, it's come
again; but I doubt it'll be the last. I've had
thoughts a' day that we wad hae a bit fine cup o'
tea owre the heid o't, and maybe a guid dram after't.
I saw Neil Jorum this morning pumping a cask o'
fine reamin Hielan whisky; and for auld lang syne he
gied me a hauf mutchkin, just out o' the measure,
afore he mixed it. I said to Neil that I wad gie my
Dick a braw surprise the nicht. But little did I ken
that he wad threaten to stick me wi' a pike, and then
gang to fecht for liberty ! Wae's me ! I'll tak back
the whisky the morn to Neil Jorum. I couldna thole·
to smell't after this nicht; it wad clean choke me.'

Maggie sat down upon a chair, and leaned her
head upon the bed, as if she were going to faint.
Dick suddenly exclaimed :

'Gudesake, it's a fearfu' nicht ! D'ye hear the
wind and the rain ?'

'Ay, ay,' said Maggie; 'it's the voice o' Liberty crying in the wilderness for ye to gang out and fecht for't.'

Dick went to the window, and opened it a little bit to get a better glimpse of the night. A gust of wind dashed the rain in his face. As he staggered back, half blinded, he said falteringly:

'It's a dreidfu' storm. I think it wad be better no to gang out the nicht.'

'And what's to come o' liberty?'

'It can wait awee,' answered Dick. 'It's waited sae lang already that a nicht or twa will no matter muckle. Liberty's gay teugh in this country. It'll neither kill nor drown. The committee canna surely expect us to gang out in a nicht like this. They maun wait till the weather clears up.'

A step was heard on the stair.

'That's young White,' said Dick in a whisper; 'he was to ca' for me. What'll I do?'

'Gang into your bed, and hap yoursel weel wi' the claes, groan nows and thans, and leave the rest to me.'

'Are ye ready, Dick?' said White, entering. 'It's time we were awa.'

'O, Andrew White,' moaned Maggie, 'is that you? This is a waefu' house. Dick is at the pint o' death.'

The lad stared as he heard Dick groan, and

turned as white as his own name. He asked what was wrong, and the distracted wife replied with tears :

'He took ill twa hours since wi' dreidfu' pains in his bowels. The doctor's been here, and he thinks it's a gane case. O dear! O dear!'

'Has he got ony physic?' asked White.

'He's got sax poothers already,' said the wife, gasping with grief, 'and if he's no better in three hours, he's to get ither seven, wi' twa blisters on the sma' o' his back, twa on his breist, and a mustard poultice mixed wi' snuff on the soles o' his feet. O my puir Richard! And, forby, the trouble is smittal.'

This was too much for White, who vanished as if the cholera was at his heels. When all was silent, Maggie laughed loud and long, while Dick leapt from bed like an acrobat, exclaiming :

'Put on the kettle, Meg, and we'll hae a stiff caulker o' toddy. Bring out the Hielan whisky!'

'And will ye no gang to fecht for liberty?'

'Liberty be—'

'Stop, Dick, nae swearing in this house. It's bad enough when I tell a thousand lees to save ye frae gaun to ruin and the gallows. Get a bit stick and mak a bleeze.'

As no other firewood could be got, Dick deliberately split up the shaft of his pike—that pike which

was to have done miracles for the rights of a down-
trodden people—and soon there was a merry fire in
the grate.   The kettle sang, and then boiled, and
then the husband and wife sat down to a feast of
steaming nectar, while the wind sobbed, and the rain
wept mournfully without.

*   *   *   *   *   *

'There's your pike, Sandy; I hae cleaned and
sharpened it wi' my ain hauns; and never be it
said that a Lattimer couldna fecht for the guid o' his
country.'

'Heeven bless ye, wife! ye've put anither heart
in me wi' thae words.   I had fears that when it cam
to the bit, ye wad flinch.'

'It's no for the dochter o' a man that suffered in
the same cause to flinch or greet like a silly tawpie.
If it had been our lot to hae bairns, it micht hae
been different—I canna tell.   As it is, I only wish
that I was a man mysel'; I wad march wi' ye to the
death.'

'But if we should fail?'

'Never fear.   I see the plan as clear as daylicht.
Ye maun succeed!   But even at the warst, though
human hauns may fail, the cause itsel', in being ane
o' truth and justice, is God's, and canna fail.'

'That's what I like to hear.   Ye mak me as bold
as a lion.   Fareweel, Jeanie, and keep your heart at

ease; for ye may depend on't that, whether we win or lose, ye'll never hear that Sandy Lattimer turned his back on the enemies o' the people. Whisht! d'ye hear that whistle? That's the signal. Now, ae kiss, and then we pairt.'

The pair embraced tenderly, and then the wife said:

'Fareweel, Sandy. Be brave, whatever ye do, and I'll wait wi' patience. Mind our bargain. Whenever I hear that ye hae ta'en Stirling Castle, I'll come east and join ye.'

'Sae be it.'

Alas!

———

CHAPTER XIX.

AT THE DEAD OF NIGHT.

'A HIDEOUS night, Alan,' said Macpherson, as the pair wound through the Drygate towards the cathedral.

'Hideous to cowards, Mac; not to us. For myself, I rather enjoy it. All you have got to do is to resign yourself to it as a thing inevitable. You will then find it quite comfortable. The worst always becomes considerably better when one knows it to be the worst. This weather will do us much service.'

'How do you make that out?'

'It will keep the Commander-in-chief and his staff in their luxurious hotels; and the rain will act as a screen to hide our movements.'

'Is that all? I wouldn't have cared a sprig of heather although it had been moonlight.'

'There is another service the night will do,' continued Alan, hardly noticing the interruption. 'It will help to damp down the mere chaff of the clubs, and leave us nothing but the solid wheat. In such a case, the wet blanket is, in its own manner, a mighty winnower.'

'Well, that's better. We shall see who comes, and how many. What number is expected?'

'It is difficult to say. There ought to be five hundred to begin with, exclusive of what Paisley may send, if it send any. But this rain will extinguish many a fire. Wouldn't it be a joke if none come at all?'

'None but our two selves. What glory would be ours! We should have the ineffable bliss in after times, when perhaps lying in our coffins or elsewhere, of thinking that we two alone were the regenerators of our country—we two, Alan Dalziel and Roderick Macpherson, of all the millions that inhabit these immortal islands. The idea transports me!'

'The idea may transport us both, if it fails, and

send different portions of our bodies into different parts of the kingdom, for the edification of an ignorant people. In this manner we should still be propagating our principles, though dead. Our dead bodies would be proclamations to the living, calling upon them to arise—to live as we lived, to fight as we fought, to die as we died.'

' Is this the Molendinar, Alan ?'

' It is none other than that famous stream ; and the bridge we are now crossing by is called the "Bridge of Sighs." '

' Ominous name !' said Macpherson, halting suddenly. ' Is there no other way to reach our rendezvous ?'

' There is, but it is somewhat of a roundabout ; and you know, Mac, that, being half across, it would be as ominous to retrace our steps. To turn your back upon a danger is just to provoke it. Forward, therefore, and the devil take superstition !'

Alan's companion moved forward accordingly, but in silence. The fact that he had crossed a' stream by a Bridge of Sighs, on so peculiar an expedition, did not at all please him. Macpherson was a hard student and a reader of hard books, and, theoretically at least, he did not believe in omens and ghosts and other popular vulgarities of the supernatural. But superstition runs in the blood as much as in the brain—there are ghosts of birth as well as ghosts of ignorance. In spite, therefore, of the dry keen scepticism of his brain, Macpherson's blood believed in signs, omens, second sight, dead candles, spectres, &c. This was because, being a born Celt, he had inherited in his flesh the effects of generations of superstition — effects which the light of knowledge and the hammers of logic were powerless to expel or destroy. You cannot wholly extinguish by training what has been bred in the bone — it must be bred out of the bone—expelled, so to say, by generations of decentralisation in marriage, education, and custom.

They had crossed the streamlet and gone a slight distance up a rugged path, when Macpherson suddenly halted, and asked under his breath:

'Did you hear a foot, Alan, as if some one were following us?'

'No,' said Alan, listening; 'your ear must have deceived you. The wind is making bagpipes of the shrubs, and to hear the sound of bagpipes is to think you hear the trampling of the clans going to harry some Lowland laird.'

'Or it may suggest the furtive footsteps of an enemy. I don't quite like this place. What a dismal gulf seems to lie beneath us! and that black mass over there?'

'That's the cathedral,' replied Alan, scanning with eager interest the grand shadowy structure,

standing so rugged and solemn in the gloom. 'Have
you been here in daylight, Mac?'

'No.'

'Or by moonlight?'

'Never!'

'You should visit it at both times. It is a magnificent sight.'

'Possibly; but to-night it is only horrible. I
don't think that I am a coward, Alan. I know that
I have walked through Hell's Glen at midnight; and
once I passed up the Devil's Staircase in Glencoe
during a snowstorm; but I never had the feeling I
have just now.'

'What feeling, you gigantic baby?'

'It is as if a cold wet hand held me—as if I were
walking among dead men's bones,' and Macpherson
shuddered as he spoke.

'That's possible enough,' said Alan; 'I have
heard that Sir William Wallace was once pursued
by five hundred English along the Bridge of Sighs,
and that he made a stand somewhere hereabouts,
and slaughtered the whole of them with his own
hand. It is said that the heroic heart of the patriot
was sustained during the fight by the choir of the
cathedral, which, so long as an Englishman remained
alive, continued to pour forth volumes of the most
wonderful music. When the last man was laid
gasping on the turf, and the warrior rested on his

reeking sword, towering amid a very mountain of
dead, the music paused for a moment, and then
gave one final burst of glory, which rang like thunder along the beautiful sinuosities of the Molendinar.
It is perhaps the bones of these Englishmen we are
standing on.'

'Come away, for Godsake!' whispered Macpherson, clutching Alan by the arm, and dragging him
forward.

'Not that way, Mac; there was a murder committed round that corner—this way.'

The Highlander followed Alan precipitately, and
for some minutes they picked their way up the hill
through the darkness and the rain, which was blown
about them in fitful gusts. They stood once more
to take breath, Macpherson listening intently with
his ear against the wind.

'What now?' said Alan; 'do you hear the foot
again?'

'I do—I am sure of it. But look!'

Alan turned towards the cathedral, upon which
his companion seemed fixedly gazing, and saw an
unexpected sight. The great pile—its vast outline
muffled in rainy gloom—appeared to be lighted up at
several points.

'It surely can't be on fire?' Alan remarked,
an uneasy feeling creeping over him for the first
time.

'No, it isn't fire—it is worse,' replied Macpherson solemnly.

'What can be worse than fire, Mac?'

'Death! These are dead lights—warnings. Let
us go home, Alan. There is ruin in this expedition
—I feel it!'

'This from you!—the man of science, the logi-
cian, the philosopher, the patriot! But I forget
—you were born at Ballachulish. It's not your
brain that speaks just now, Mac—it's your blood.
Feeling and tradition are still too much for knowledge.'

'Don't jest, Alan. What you say may be true;
but if you had—Good heavens! See!'

Alan turned again, and saw that one of the
lights had mounted to the tower of the cathedral.
It seemed to be carried by a shadowy figure that
waved its arms in the wind, as if it were warning or
imploring.

'Will you believe that, Alan?'

'Why, yes, I can believe what I see; but I don't
see any use in misconstruing it. I tell you what,
Mac; I believe that the light we see is a signal, and
that we are being betrayed. I suspect that a party
of soldiers are bivouacking in the cathedral for some
purpose or another. Let us hurry forward and warn
our friends.'

Macpherson did not believe his companion's in-

terpretation of the fiery phenomenon they had seen;
but nevertheless he followed, and in a very short
time they reached the summit of the ravine, where
they stood and looked back at the cathedral. But
the lights were gone, and Alan said :

'It's like a dream.'

'A warning vision, Alan, that's what it is.'

They resumed their journey, and were passing a
little copse, when a man started into the middle of
the way, presented a pike, and cried,

'Who goes there ?'

'Friends,' replied Alan.

'By what token ?' demanded the outpost.

'Bannockburn,' was Alan's reply.

'All right; pass on, and be quick; they are
met.'

In a few minutes the two Radicals reached the
place of meeting, where they found assembled a party
of perhaps forty or fifty men, armed with pikes, guns,
and sticks ready to receive pike-heads. It was a
solemn meeting. The men stood in groups conversing on the subject which lay like a weight at
their hearts. They were evidently ill at ease —
shocked at the smallness of the number who had
obeyed the summons of the Central Committee.
Hundreds were expected to appear at Germiston,
the spot whereon they now stood; but to think that
not more than fifty at the most should have come,

was a blow which, combined with the dismalness of
the night, produced a feeling of the most intense
discouragement. Occurring at this exact juncture
of their proceedings, it was worse than a defeat. The
general impression was, that the foul weather had
cooled the ardour of the warriors whose rhetorical
heroism they knew so well; and their apparent cowardice drew forth many a deep-mouthed curse. As
Dalziel and Macpherson approached the conspirators,
Andrew Hardie stepped forward and gave them a
hearty welcome.

'Why, what's the meaning of this, Hardie? Why
are there so few? Where are the hundreds that
were expected to be here, armed to the teeth?'

'That's what we've been trying to guess, Mr.
Dalziel, for the last ten minutes. But we're a' in
the dark, like yoursel'. When I cam here, I expected to see as mony as would at least hae made
three regiments; and I was mair than stunned to
see only thae—hardly as mony as wad stop a hole
in a hedge. It's no fair. There should hae been
the Anderston Lancers, the Black Watch frae the
Gorbals, the Calton Cleavers, the Brigton Bruisers,
the Ruglen Rangers, the Brigade of Wiseacres frae
the 'Shaws, the Paisley Fire-eaters, the Kir'ntilloch
Scalpers, and the Riflers frae Cam'slang. Had a'
thae come, we micht hae marched to certain victory.
Wi' a haunfu' like this, victory's no possible. I've

a guid mind to gang hame, and let the Committee fecht their ain battles.'

'I fear, Alan,' remarked Macpherson, 'that your words about the weather winnowing our forces are like to prove destructively true. The rain has washed away whole regiments of chaff.'

'And left only twa-three genuine pickles like oursels,' remarked a man named Henderson; 'but ye ken what King Harry the Fifth says in the play: "If we are marked to die, we are enough to do our country loss; and if we live, the fewer men the greater share of honour." Think on that view o' the case, Hardie, and ne'er speak o' gaun hame to your saft bed, when sae mony puir folk are in a condition o' stark misery for want o' their richts. Let us march, I say! My voice is still for war, like the man in Addison's Greek play.'

'Do you hear that, Mac?' said Alan; 'our comrade has been plunging into the English classics.'

'Heels-o'er-head. But here come two messengers in haste.'

'Weel, men, what news?' asked Hardie; 'whaur's the rest o' the forces that should hae been here? It's past eleven.'

'There's great news,' replied one of the men, named Turner, exultingly; 'England is up in arms, and now is the time for Scotland to strike a corresponding blow. You must march at once.'

'Very good, Turner,' said Hardie; 'but whaur's a' the companies that were to meet here? Answer that first!'

'That is easily answered,' said Turner's companion, who was closely muffled in a traveller's cloak, and seemed a stranger. 'The news from England has altered our plans slightly. The Paisley men have marched to attack Dumbarton Castle, which will be in their hands before to-morrow dawns. We have sent a company to Hamilton to coöperate with the men there in an attack upon the London mail. Another corps has gone out by Kirkintilloch to proceed by Kilsyth towards Carron; and for the same purpose a band has been sent by Airdrie. You will proceed by Condorret and Cumbernauld, and unite with the others at Bonnybridge, from which you will move on Carron in force. With the cannon got at Carron, you will strike straight at Stirling Castle, within the walls of which we have several good friends, who will put the fortress into your hands. By this time the Radical forces will be augmented a thousandfold, and your crowning blow will then be delivered against Edinburgh Castle, where we have also a number of secret friends and trusty allies, who are smoothing the way for the approach of the patriot army. My only regret is, that I cannot accompany you to-night. We are working hard to perfect the arrangements for the proclamation of the Provisional

Government. By to-morrow evening, however, I hope to join you under the walls of Stirling, and take part in the assault. In the mean time, I bid you God speed! Be bold, and success will attend you. Let this be your watchword—" God and our Right!" '

This speech was delivered with great energy, and in the manner of a popular orator. The Radicals responded to it with a cheer, which was not, however, entirely unanimous. A few remained silent, perhaps suspicious that the import of the harangue was too good to be exactly true.

'I say, Alan, there is too much rosewater in that man's speech. There is something in the aspect of affairs that I don't like.'

'What would you have, Mac? A general will always make rousing speeches. It would never do to dishearten the forces, and send them into battle with trembling hearts. A soldier should never be allowed to believe in the impossible.'

'Yet my heart misgives me.'

'My dear Macpherson,' said Alan solemnly, 'if these secret apprehensions of yours are really uncontrollable, it would be better for you to go back. Keep close to your lodgings for a few days, and watch how the storm blows. As for myself, I'll see this matter to the end. If it were hopeless to go forward, going back would be to me still more hopeless. I must go on.'

Macpherson did not reply, but stood silent and sullen, undecided apparently what course to pursue. Remembering the part he had taken in the Radical agitation, he was ashamed to turn back; yet the superstition of his nature, invincible to reason and logic, and excited by certain ominous circumstances, made him afraid to proceed with the perilous expedition. Perhaps, too, the difference between making splendid speeches and receiving loud applause under the cover of some roof, and handling the cold shaft of a pike, or the barrel of a gun, on a dark night, in a lonely field, and amid a tempest of rain, struck both these young fellows in an unexpected manner, and gave them undescribable sensations. It is hard to believe that Alan had no misgivings; but if he had, he concealed them under clouds of bitterness and cynical humour.

'You know, Mac,' he said, 'that these warriors couldn't well proceed without a doctor to bind up the wounds they may receive in collision with the enemy. I have, therefore, the argument of humanity urging me onward, in addition to that of patriotism. Heaven help us! It is a dark expedition at the best. But enterprises worse begun have before now brought glory to the actors.'

'And sometimes gibbets.'

'That possibility dogs the meanest adventures; and it is the mean enterprise that makes the mean

death. The scaffold is absolute fame in a cause like
ours, unless I have misread history. The martyrs
are the kings of freedom.'

'And its victims,' repeated Macpherson, unable
to throw off the terrible shadow of the scaffold and
the axe.

'Say no more, Roderick. With that fatalistic
mood of yours, it is impossible that you can pierce
the inevitable darkness of the present moment. A
few days probably will blow the cloud from your
mind, when you may see things in a new light. But
what's this? Can they be quarrelling?'

'Well, gentlemen,' the muffled stranger was saying, 'there need be no quarrelling about that. Whoever has doubts is not compelled to march, and may
go back to the city. It is to be hoped, however, that
all who return will keep strictly silent regarding what
they know and have seen.'

'That is nae mair than fair,' remarked Henderson; 'and in order to bring things to a head, I propose that them that's no willing to gang should
staun on the left haun, and them that intend to stick
to the cause should staun on the richt.'

'Like the goats and the sheep,' whispered Alan
to his friend. This separation was at once made by
the two parties filing into their respective places.
Over thirty resolved to march, while the rest hung
aloof, dissatisfied with the extent and appearance of

the gathering, as well as with the explanation given
by the stranger.   Alan was glad to find that Macpherson came with him to the warlike side of the
field, although it was too dark for Alan to see the
cloud of trouble that veiled his companion's face.
As soon as the separation was completed, the stranger
spoke.

'Now, gentlemen, it only remains for me to inform you that a scout has been sent on before you
to rouse the villages on your line of march; so that,
as you advance, the tramp of your patriotic feet will
make adherents spring from the earth to join the
liberators of their country.   I may also inform you
that, during the first part of the march, which ex-
tends to the village of Condorret, you will be under
the command of Mr. Andrew Hardie, a good soldier
and a tried patriot—one who has already defied the
brutality of authority in protecting from destruction
the proclamation of the Committee.   At Condorret,
on account of the augmentation of your forces, some
rearrangement of the command will be necessary;
but you will find a gentleman there who will give
you all needful information.   I am glad also to be
able to say, that in one of the most consistent and
strenuous of your members you have a most accom-
plished surgeon.   Need I say that I refer to Mr.
Alan Dalziel?   He is known to you all as a young
man of great promise; and I sincerely trust that the

events of this great and memorable campaign will be
to him but the beginning of a glorious career.'

This elicited genuine marks of approbation; for
Alan was greatly liked among the Radicals, as a
political enthusiast of the purest and most unselfish
type. The simple fact that he had been in the habit
of visiting and aiding the distressed made him known
privately to the Radicals and their wives and children, to whom he was thus peculiarly endeared.

'Do you hear that, Alan?' asked his friend.
'You have become famous before you have struck
a blow.'

'Here, Hardie,' said Turner, 'is the half of a
card, the corresponding half of which you will find
in the possession of a gentleman at Condorret. You
and he will arrange about the command of the united
forces. Farewell till to-morrow; and the Spirit of
Liberty be with you!'

'Thank you, sir,' replied Hardie, who then turned
to the Radicals, who were preparing to move, and
said, 'Hear me, men, for one moment. This is a
dangerous expedition we are about to enter upon;
but as I believe it to be a just one, I accept my post
with all its consequences. Let the worst come to the
worst, we have the consolation of the great heroes of
old—we fight in a righteous cause. Onward, then,
to victory! In the words of the address, let us swear
to return in triumph, or return no more!'

VOL. III.   P

' We swear !'

The deep oath sounded through the dismal night as the Radicals, grasping their pikes and guns, marched away to their unknown doom. The party who had shown the white feather, or were wise, then returned stealthily to their homes in the city.

CHAPTER XX.

UNMASKED.

FIVE minutes after both parties disappeared, two figures emerged from behind some bushes, and one said to the other,

' Well, Captain, did you ever see such consummate folly ?   I shall remember this sight as long as I live.'

' You may well do that, Semple.   It is only once in a life-time that such stupendous idiotcy is exhibited by men otherwise rational, although I have seen something of the same kind before.'

' But they were nipped in the bud then.'

' This time, they will be blasted in the blossom. Come away, Andrew, we have seen the beginning of the end.'

'Hush, Captain, somebody comes this way. Let us hide!'

'It is too late. Stand.'

At this moment three persons—two men and a woman—advanced towards Andrew Semple and Captain Batwing. One of the new arrivals spoke :

'Would ye tell us, gentlemen, whether ye've seen a company o' men hereabout the nicht?'

'By Jove! Captain,' whispered Andrew, 'this is Fox the twister. I owe the meddlesome goose a twist, and I've a good mind to thraw his neck.'

'Be quiet a little. Yes, sir, we have seen a company of men, but they have gone.'

'D'ye ken whaur they've gane to? Are they far aff?'

'They are too far away for you to overtake them,' answered the Captain.

'But not too far off to escape the gallows,' added Andrew; 'they think themselves that they have gone to glory, but *I* think that they have only gone to perdition, which is good enough for fools.'

'In that case it wad fit you to a nicety. It's lang since ye've been ripe for a het corner down by, I ken by the rattle o' your tongue, that sounds for a' the worl' like rotten pease in a blether.'

'Gentlemen,' said the lady who accompanied Pate Fox, 'do not quarrel. All we want to know is whether you can give us any information about the persons who were lately here—who they were, and whither they have gone ? If you cannot help us we can retire.'

' Stop !' said Semple suddenly, and looking keenly and wickedly at the lady ; ' I can give you some information. The fellows you refer to are traitors and conspirators ; and they have marched away somewhere to overthrow the Government. They expect to succeed ; but I know they will fail ; and if they fail, there is nothing for them but the rope and the axe. Further, I can tell the name of one of them. He is a little bit of a lawyer, a little less of a doctor, a great goose, a rank fool, and a base bastard, and his name is—Alan Dalziel !'

' Sir,' said Christine Dundas—for it was she who accompanied Pate and the other person who had not yet spoken—' Sir, Alan Dalziel is a gentleman, and you are—'

' Well, what am I ?'

' Only Andrew Semple—one who meanly betrayed Dalziel, and tried to supplant him. Come away, Mr. Fox. There is no good to be found here.'

' Do take her away, Mr. Peter Fox, twister—do take her away, you precious fatherly cavalier. There is no chance of seeing her bastard lover to-night, nor to-morrow either, nor next day, nor even the day after. She will see him dancing elegantly at the end of a rope before long, or I am mistaken.'

'Ye scoun'rel,' said Pate, in a rage, 'a rape wad fit you; and if ye dinna stop that monkey jaw o' yours, I'll knock your rotten teeth down your dirty thrapple.'

'You foul grizzly-beard,' replied Semple, flaming, 'I owe you a debt, and I'll pay you now with interest;' and he rushed madly at Pate, who would inevitably have gone down in the encounter. But that other person who had hitherto remained silent met the charge, by giving Semple a tremendous smash right between the eyes, which sent him whirling into a little lake of mud that had lain there for years, evidently waiting its proper tenant.

'Take that, you scum of the world!'

'Come, come, gentlemen,' interposed Captain Batwing; 'two to one is not quite fair. Enough of this.'

'And who are you?' asked the hero who had so neatly levelled Semple, and who was no other than Jules Elmar, whom the reader may remember; 'who are you that would stand by there and see your base jack-snipe insult a lady without stopping his lying mouth? Who are you, I say?'

'It does not concern you who I am,' returned the Captain, leaning more old-man-like upon his staff, 'you had better move off; it will be safer; I am armed.'

'You are armed, are you? So am I, and I can

hit a nail at twenty paces with the best in the city. But I think I have heard your voice and seen your figure before. Let me see your face—let me see—O ho! a beard of sixty and a brow of forty; how is this?'

'Stand back, sir!'

'No, sir, I won't—there! It's a false beard,' and Elmar plucked the beard from the face of the Captain, who stood straight up, quite a different-looking person from the decrepit old man of a minute before. Quick as lightning he drew a pistol and fired in the face of Elmar, who, however, quicker than lightning, struck up the arm of the would-be assassin, whose own jaw the bullet ploughed deeply. The man dropped his pistol and stood groaning helplessly before his antagonist. Christine gave a cry of alarm, and said,

'Surely, Jules, you have not shot him.'

'No, no; it was his own confounded pistol, with which he attempted to shoot me. I simply knocked it up, and off it went in the proper direction. Let me look at the fellow without his beard—Richmond the spy, by heaven!'

'Richmond!' exclaimed Pate.

'Richmond!' whispered Christine, shivering at the revelation.

'No other—that very Captain Batwing whom I have watched prowling about the city like a loathsome bird of the night. You have got a mark, sir;

your jaw is grazed; and it will be a jaw to you as long as you live. Every time you look in your mirror, you will be reminded of this night, and of the miserable, despicable work in which you have been engaged. Nay; if it be true that men resume their bodies at the resurrection, you will bear that mark through all the ages of eternity—an endless mark of infamy!'

'Stop, Jules,' said Christine with feeling; 'no more of that. The man is sufficiently punished.'

'Ay, ay,' added Pate; 'it's eneugh. Nae mair jibes.'

'I pity you, sir,' Christine said, addressing Richmond. 'I never did or wished you any harm, and I would rather have suffered myself than seen you in that state.'

'Thank you, lady,' spoke the spy with difficulty; 'and I never did or wished *you* any harm either.'

'But where is Alan?' she asked.

'I am sorry,' was the reply, 'that such as he should have gone with the Radicals. But whatever I may have done, that was his own affair, with which I have had nothing to do. Let me tell you honestly, however, that he is in the deepest danger.'

'O, how can he be saved?' was all that she could murmur.

'There is only one who might save him,' Richmond said with evident sincerity.

' Who is it ?'

' Lord Carmyle. I have heard that Dalziel once
saved his lordship's life. Now, his lordship has
some power in this affair. Go to him at once—to-
morrow—and urge him to befriend you. Lady, as
God is in heaven, it is my best wish that you may
succeed.'

' Thank you, sir—thank you, thank you. I shall
take your advice. But before we go away let me
bind your wound.'

Richmond sat upon a bank, upon the wet grass,
and under the shelter of a tree, amazed, but rather
pleased than otherwise, as that gentle creature dexterously and tenderly bound his bleeding face. He
felt like one who is dreaming a painful yet not un-
pleasant dream.

' God bless you,' he whispered, when she had
finished her kindly act of surgery. ' Alan is a brave
lad; and when you save him, as I feel confident you
will do, you will make him a brave good wife. It
will be well with you both.'

' And you ?' she asked, almost pathetically.

' Never cloud your memory with my name. I
am a broken man—self-destroyed—ruined by pride
and a false ambition.'

Richmond now hung his head, as Christine, Pate,
and Elmar moved silently away. He seemed quite
crushed by the weight of his wretched thoughts, and

sat plucking the grass, utterly careless of the inclemency of the night. By and by, however, a lame, dirty, and savage-looking figure, presumably that of Andrew Semple, crawled towards him out of the gloom; and they both stumbled home, mentally stunned and physically pained, like twin-spirits of desolation.

CHAPTER XXI.

WARNINGS.

DAY was beginning to break as the Radical army entered the village of Condorret. It was a melancholy dawn, and the patriots were a melancholy spectacle. The rain had largely decreased, but great masses of cloud still hung heavily in heaven, behind them, towards the west. Some of those clouds broke over Glasgow in such enormous deluges, that, in consequence, the Radical movement was practically extinguished in the city. Many fiery intentions, which were to have blazed up on this particular day, the 5th April 1820, or 'Wat Wansday,' as it was called, were drowned out by the providential interposition of the weather. Hundreds of pike-warriors leapt from their beds at the first sound of the chanticleerian bugle; but on seeing the black streaming sky, and hearing the music of the gurgling gutters, they crept back to their soft beds or hard boards until such times as the weather might clear up, and render rebellion a more pleasant exercise. But the meteorological gods were relentless. All day long the wind blew and the rain poured, and effectively imprisoned the Radicals within walls of water. Indeed, the writer has been assured by men who lived then, that Glasgow was saved from pillage and massacre by that rain-tempest.

Fortunately, the Radicals who marched from Glasgow on the previous night had now almost passed beyond the present rain-zone. It is true that the whole western arch of the sky was still black with ponderous cloud-masses, and that, far to the south, they still heard, as they had heard all night, the divine utterances of the thunder-spirit, as if he were engaged delivering judgment and imposing penalties. But in the east, the clouds were broken and scattered, pierced and routed by the silver-speared couriers of the sun. Now and then, a lark, the little gray prophet of the dawn, springing from his couch of liquid gems, would soar under the wing of a brooding cloud, and melt his passionate soul in melodious adoration. These signs were sweet to the weary warriors, as they trudged into the village, and they hoped that they would have a pleasant day.

Hope of some kind was needed, for things had occurred during the march which were extremely

discouraging. They began their journey with nearly
forty rank and file; when day began to break, Hardie
and Alan discovered that their numbers were now
reduced to less than thirty. The fact is that almost
every half-mile since they had sworn, amid the shadows of Germiston wood, to return in triumph, or
return no more, some patriot, becoming timid, probably under the cooling influences of the drenching
night, had dropped quietly out of the ranks, and
crept home to his bed.

But what cut Alan most was the defection of
Macpherson, who had not proceeded a mile towards
glory when his superstitious feelings completely over-
mastered him. He confessed to Alan, almost with
tears in his eyes, that he could not go any farther;
and Alan, believing that his friend was no coward in
the base sense, bade him farewell with the pain of
sincere sorrow. Each believed that he would never
see the other again—and neither they did. This incident had a saddening effect upon Alan. It made
him more meditative, less communicative, and less
hopeful regarding the enterprise. He did not flinch,
however, but marched along with a dogged self-will,
and a secret desire to find the best or endure the
worst. Curious apprehensions began to show their
black visages at the windows of his reason; but he
shut them out with thick curtains of cynical and
egotistic bitterness.

At length the army of liberation halted at Condorret for an early breakfast, and to hold a council of war. They were met by King, Captain Batwing's chief lieutenant, who was the scout that had been sent out to rouse the villages on the line of march. He had lodged with John Baird all night, and was now about to push forward to complete his mission as bearer of the 'Fiery Cross.' He and Baird, Hardie and Dalziel, met in a small room of a publichouse, in another apartment of which the main body of the army was also accommodated. After consuming some whisky and a piece of oat-cake, the four put their heads profoundly together.

'In the first place,' began Hardie, 'I have here the hauf o' a card.'

'And I have another half,' said King; 'put them together, Baird, and see if they correspond.'

'To a letter,' Baird remarked, after testing the bits of paper.

'Now, then,' Hardie resumed briskly, 'I here lay down my commission, and it remains to appoint my successor in the chief command.'

'As that successor,' said King, 'I have authority from the committee in Glasgow to propose Mr. Baird, who is known for a keen Radical, a man of soldierly genius, and, what is of great importance in this part of the expedition, he is possessed of a thorough knowledge of the topography of the country. You, Hardie,

if you are not unwilling, are to be next in command.
What say you?'

'I am content. I couldna wish to serve under a
better chief.'

'Thank you,' responded Baird. 'I could hae
been willing to serve under you, Hardie; but as it
has been decreed itherwise, I accept the appointment.
It is an honour which I hope I won't disgrace this
day, whatever be the upshot.'

Alan, speaking for the first time, asked, 'And
what is the number of your forces here, Baird? I
have heard that you have a brave company.'

'We *had* a brave company, Mr. Dalziel; but I
am sorry to say that some enemy or devil has got
amongst us, so that this morning I can muster no
more than half a dozen good fellows.'

This announcement staggered them all, except
King, who rose and said cheerfully,

'No matter, gentlemen; our number will be
sufficiently powerful before we make the assault on
Carron. I must now go forward to rouse Camelon
and Falkirk; and I expect that you will follow with
all speed. Remember, we meet at Bonnybridge.'

In fifteen minutes the Radicals, augmented by
six, were again on the march.

They had just reached the outskirts of the village
when they were overtaken by a young girl, half-
dressed, her hair streaming in the wind. She fell

upon Baird's breast, and burst out in passionate exclamation,

'O John, John! ye're surely no gaun. O, stay at hame! I dreamed a waefu' dream yestreen. I thought I saw ye lying deid in a bluidy sheet, and the sogers staunin owre ye with drawn swords. O, John, for my sake bide at hame! bide at hame!'

This was Baird's sweetheart, and the sight of the spectacle almost unmanned Hardie and Dalziel, both of whom had left their hearts in Glasgow. They turned away, and moved forward, deeply distressed.

'Mary, Mary,' Baird murmured, 'what brings ye here? D'ye mind what ye promised yestreen? Ye were bold then.'

'But my dream—my fearfu' dream!'

'Dreams are aye contrar. Gang hame, my dearie, and hae nae fear. In three months, Mary, ye'll be mine,' and the pale commander kissed the frightened girl, who hung despairingly upon his neck. Having gently released himself, Mary stood helpless in the middle of the road, looking wistfully at her lover. She could only say—and she spoke like one in a dream—

'O, John! in three months, ye'll be mine, and I'll be yours; but it'll no be in this life.'

Long after Baird was out of sight, the girl stood on the road looking after him. In turning a corner, he looked back, and saw her still there, pale and

beautiful, and more like a spirit than a human creature. His heart almost burst in his body, and if it
had not been for Hardie and Alan, who caught hold
of him on each side, he would either have fallen to
the ground, or gone back.

A mile farther on they reached a spring of clear
water; and, as they stopped to drink, an old woman
stepped suddenly from behind a bush and confronted
Baird.

'Elsie!' he exclaimed, astonished to see the old
woman so early afoot.

'Ay, just Elsie,' the woman replied, fastening
two glowing eyes upon him. 'John Baird, I hae
warned ye ance, and I hae warned ye twice, and now
I hae risen lang afore my hour to warn ye for the
third and last time! D'ye ken what I mean?'

'Ay, ay, Elsie. Ye mean weel, but I doubt ye're
wrang. Here's a penny, gang back to your bed, and
tak a guid sleep.'

'Keep your siller to yoursel', John Baird —
ye'll need it a'. Then ye *will* gang to your ain
ruin?'

'Hoots, no, Elsie, my woman; there's nae ruin
in the case. Guid-morning t'ye.'

'Stay, John Baird. D'ye mind the Woman o'
Badenheath?'

Baird turned pale as he answered the question:
'Yes, Elsie, I mind.'

' And wha was't that prophesee't she wad neithe
dee in her bed nor dee on the yerth ?'

' Weel, Elsie, it was you.'

' And tell me, how did she dee ?'

' She dee't in the air, Elsie—she hang't hersel'.'

' Just sae—and Elsie was a true prophet.   Tel
me again, John Baird, what was the doom o' bonni
Annie Raeburn ?'

' Dinna come owre that story, Elsie, for pity'
sake !'

' I maun, though—I maun come owre't for you
sake.   What was Annie's doom, I say ?'

' Elsie, Elsie, she raise in the nicht-time, when
she was a bride, within three days o' her waddin',
and walkit sleepin' into the loch, and was drowned.'

' And wha was't that foretauld and aftertauld it ?
Tell me that !'

' It was you, Elsie, it was you !'

' Ay, it was me.   I kent that bonnie Annie was
a sleep-walker, and that she likit weel to wander by
the loch-side, and even paidle in't wi' her bare white
feet.   I warn't them to watch her, but they wadna be
warn't, and only made licht o' auld gangrel Elsie.
Then it cam' at last, and I saw her gang into the
loch, though I was sleepin' as soun' as hersel'.   It's
true, I tell ye, as Heeven's abin !   At the deid hour
o' the nicht, when my een were steekit and sneckit
and dooble lockit wi' the heavy hauns o' sleep, I saw

the bonnie burd as plain's I see you, gaun slow on her ain wee pearlins o' feet, wi' naething on but her nicht sarkie, white as the munebeam—I saw her gang into the loch, and wade and wade, till, like a gliff o' licht, she gaed down wi' a screich into the Deid Man's Hole; and I wauken't wi' the cauld sweat staunin' on my brow like blabs o' dew. And I gaed and tauld them whaur to seek for the sweet wanner't lammie. And whaur did they get her? Tell me that, John Baird!'

'E'en as ye say, Elsie, in the Deid Man's Hole. But it's time we were awa.'

'Bide awhilie yet, John. Tell me ae thing mair, for ye're auld eneugh to mind the story o' wee mitherless Willie—Willie Elphin, ye ken, wha gaed amissin, and wasna fand for twa years. Ye may weel grue, John Baird. But did I no aye say that Willie wad be fan some day, and how he wad be fan? And how was that? Did I no prophesee that he wad come hame, but no in the flesh? Now, tell me how he cam' hame?'

'Lordsake! Elsie, ye wad fricht the de'il himsel' wi' your stories!'

'Maybe; but how cam' Willie hame?'

'Ye ken weel eneugh already. They got his puir wee deid body in the benmost bore o' an auld pit.'

'Ay, John; but how?' persisted the old woman, as Baird hesitated.

'They got naething but his banes,' said Baird, with a shiver, 'and they were bleached as white as caulk.'

'That's the true story, John. I said he wad come hame, but no in the flesh, and there wasna a bit flesh about his white, white banes; and wha proved that it was the very banes o' the wee wanner't bairn?'

'It was you again, Elsie; but how the deevel ye kent, naebody could understand. The folk ca'd ye a witch.'

'Ay, did they; they ca'd me a witch, and waur nor that. But I'm no a witch, nor a warlock either —no, nor even a prophet. Yet ye see, John Baird, that I ken things; ay, and I ken mair things nor ye think o'. I hear what ye canna hear, I see what ye canna see; and I tell ye that ye're gaun to ruin. It's no for naething that I hae dreams and visions. Ye may smile, but did ye ever ken me wrang when I said onything?'

'Gudesake, no, Elsie; but hae dune. We've stoppit owre lang already.'

'Ye'll no hae muckle langer to bide, if ye like to gang on after what I tell ye. I've seen ye in the spirit, John, in a vision, and it aye haunts me. It cam first at nicht, but now it comes at a' times; when I'm gaun owre the muir, or in the moss amang the peats, or when I'm in the wud gatherin' sticks,

it comes on me like a flaught o' lichtnin'. And
what do I see? I see twa men on a high place—
I'll no name't—wi' twa-three ither men about them,
ane o' them like a minister and ane o' them leanin'
on an axe, wi' something black on his face. Aside
the twa men twa somethings hing doon wi' loops
at the ends o' them, and far below I catch a sicht
o' a hale sea o' tearfu' faces, and there's a low
moanin' voice comes to my ear, as if somebody were
deid or gaun to dee.' Elsie paused a moment, keeping her eye fixed on Baird, while a singularly
pathetic change came over her manner. 'O, John
Baird!' she resumed, 'hear me for the last time.
Ane o' the men I saw staunin' on that dreidfu' stage,
below ane o' the loops, was yoursel'! Your very
sel', I say, as sure as the Lord's in Heeven! I saw
ye as plain as I see ye the now, and your hauns
were tied at your side. Tak' warnin', and dinna
gang wi' thae men. Gang back, gang back while it
is yet time; gang back to your ain peacefu' hame;
gang back to the love o' your mither; gang back to
the arms o' your ain bonnie Mary; gang back, O
gang back to safety and salvation!'

Elsie's eyes glowed with a most unnatural light,
as she concluded her passionate appeal to Baird,
whom she continued to watch with painful intensity.
Hardie, who had been standing apart, listening im-
patiently to the ravings of Elsie, now advanced to

put an end to the colloquy. He said with some warmth,

'Lordsake, Baird, this'll never do; you must not let the campaign be spoilt by the silly visions of a doited granniewitch. Come on!'

'Wha are ye that speak?' demanded Elsie, starting, as Hardie's face caught her eye.

'Wha I am matters naething to you,' Hardie replied.

'But muckle, muckle to yoursel', my braw soger-birkie; for ye're the ither figure I saw aside John Baird, staunin' below the ither loop. O man, but if ye had sense, ye wad gang back, and tak' Baird and the rest wi' ye. Fling a' your pikes in the sheugh and gang hame, and ye'll bless auld Else a' the days o' your life.'

'Thank ye, Elsie,' said Baird, by no means untouched by the woman's strange assault. Had Baird been alone, he would inevitably have gone back; and so would each of the corps, had each been alone. But in their corporate capacity they dared not confess how much the ill-omened language of the prophetess had secretly impressed them. Each felt the white feather fluttering in his heart, but the exhibition of it, either by word or act, they dreaded more than even the words of this wrinkled apparition, who might, after all, be only uttering the merest fumes of madness. 'Thank ye, Elsie; ye hae spoken for

our guid, nae doubt; but each kens his ain ken.
We're gaun awa on a great mission, Elsie, and naething maun hinder us. Duty abin a', let death come
when or in what form it may. Fareweel. Fa' in,
men!'

'Is't even sae?' said the old woman sadly. 'Ye'll
no tak' my advice? Weel, John Baird, I've had a
mission too, as ye ca't, and I've finished it. Ye
maun a' dree your ain weird; it's at your elbow and
ye dinna see't; but ye'll mind my words afore the
mune is auld. As for mysel', I'll gang hame and
greet.'

The Radicals now marched eastward, medita-
tively silent, leaving Elsie leaning on her crutch.
Alan lingered behind, feeling a strange interest in
the withered oracle, whose words had stirred his
imagination profoundly.

'Farewell, Elsie,' he said softly, 'I for one don't
despise your words.'

Elsie, looking up, gazed at Alan for a whole
minute without speaking. At length she said,

'Young sir, the best way no to despise words o'
wisdom is to obey them. But ye're no gaun to obey
them.'

'I'll bear them in mind, however, and not mis-
spend any chance of life or safety.'

'It's no the first chance ye've mis-spent. But
what brought *you* here? Ye're no ane o' them,'

and she pointed to the disappearing company; 'ye may think wi' them, but ye dinna belang to them, and ye shouldna be here. Ye'll maybe think me daft or a witch? It maks nae matter; I've been lang used to ill names—they dinna hurt me, though I hae seen better days. But d'ye hear, young gentleman, put spurs to your horse, and ride hame—hame—hame!'

'Elsie, I have neither horse nor home.'

'Nae horse and nae hame?' and she clutched him suddenly by the hand, and looked wildly into his eyes; 'let me tell you that the horse aye comes to the gallant rider; sae ye'll no wait lang for a horse, and ye'll ride hame, for ye hae a hame—a hame ye never saw, and somebody ye never saw waits and wearies for ye there. Ay, ay, my bonnie lad, I ken things, I see things, and I see in your e'e that ye hae baith a hame and braw freens. Ye'll hae to ride fast, though, and never look ahint—sink the rowels deep, and gallop owre moss and muir—awa to the south; and there's a braid river, and—' she dropped his hand suddenly, and added distractedly, 'but some o' yon misguided chiels will never see their hame ony mair!—never ony mair!—never ony mair! It's waefu'—waefu'—waefu'!'

Elsie fixed her eyes on space, and became apparently totally unconscious of Alan's presence. Alan therefore turned away sadly, believing that

Elsie's brain was unhinged; and as he knew that some kinds of mania take a prophetic form, he was not surprised at the peculiar colour of her wanderings. Whatever was her mental condition, she now stood rooted to the ground like a Fate, on the edge of the crystal well.

       *   *   *   *   *   *

Forward! forward!

CHAPTER XXII.

BATTLE OF BONNYMUIR.

So forward the Radicals went, rather moody and melancholy. They were brooding over the singular warnings of old Elsie, and wondering whether her words would on this occasion come true, as her vaticinations had so often done before.

But neither melancholy, nor apprehension, nor even fear can wholly extinguish hunger, so that when the little army reached Castlecary-bridge, across the Forth and Clyde Canal, the thought that most filled the mind of each of them was how he might get something to make a meal of. Freedom, honour, and glory are excessively important affairs, every

one of them; but they are baubles to the hungry.
There are some rare mortals who are capable of
starving for an idea; but the majority of mankind
must eat. Nor is there anything indecent in this.
Good eating has high moral and intellectual bear-
ings. A well-fed man is more likely to be a better
man than one who is starved or fed on the husks of
things; and certainly, plenty of meat and good must
help to make good soldiers. This fact, known to
all commanders, was not unknown to Baird and
Hardie, who called a halt in front of a grocer's shop
on the north bank of the canal, and fed their men
on bread and porter. It was, however, a scanty meal,
though it was all they could afford.

The honest grocer who supplied the provisions
was astonished at the appearance of his customers,
armed as they were with pikes and muskets. They
looked wind-battered, rain-soaked, weary and pallid,
and altogether unpolished. The glitter of the soldier was not about them, yet they seemed soldiers of
a sort. Of what sort, was soon made evident to the
merchant by Hardie, who said,

'Now, Mr. Buchanan'—that was the man's name
—'what is the damage?'

'Eight shillings neat, but I'll be content with
seven-and-six.'

'That's a rather serious sum in the present
state of our military chest,' Henderson interposed;

'perhaps Mr. Buchanan would accept a bill for the
amount at six months' date, to be drawn upon the
Provisional Government now established at Glasgow ?'

'Wi' a' respect, gentlemen,' the landlord replied,
'I hae nae faith in that kind o' paper. The image
o' King Geordie is the only acceptable clink at Castle-
cary Brig. Your Provisional Government can get
nae tick here.'

'Ye're no feart,' said Hardie, smiling faintly, and
rattling his pike on a stone.

'No ae bit, atweel,' answered the landlord good-
naturedly, yet with a touch of defiance in his voice.
'I see that ye're Radicals, but I'm mista'en if that
means rascals; sae, ye'll be kind enough, I'm sure,
to pay me in guid hard siller. Ae bird o' that kind
in the haun is worth twa in ony Provisional bush.'

The sum was at length paid by Baird, at whose
request Buchanan gave a receipt, which the Radicals
themselves probably intended to present to the Provisional Government for repayment. As the re-
freshed warriors were leaving, the landlord whispered
in Baird's ear,

'I've nae richt to ken whaur you and your comrades are gaun, or what ye're after; but I wish ye
nae ill, and I wad like to gie ye a hint.'

'What is't?'

'The 10th Hussars are stationed at Kilsyth, and
it's my opinion that they're on the alert for some-

body. Tak' my advice, and get into some quiet hole
without ony mair ado.'

'D'ye tak' us for moudiewarts?' asked Baird in-
dignantly.

'If I did, I wad ca' ye political moudiewarts; but
I say solemnly, that if ye dinna tak' my advice, ye're
na better than deid men.'

'Nae fears,' replied Baird. 'Let the Hussars
come; we're ready for them! Forward! forward!'

After marching a short distance the commanders
divided their forces; the larger division, under Baird,
marching along the canal bank, and the rest, under
Hardie, proceeding by the highway. Hardie's party
were in some sense foragers. They were scant of
arms, and in order to supply themselves, they visited
a farm-house or two, and appropriated a fowling-
piece and a hayfork. One blunder in tactics, however, they committed. Among others, they met a
dragoon riding to join his regiment at Kilsyth. Instead of disarming him, and making him a prisoner
of war, they let him proceed. They gave him also
a copy of the Radical address, which of course, like
a loyal subject, he carried to head-quarters at the top
of his speed. This, with the intelligence given by
the soldier, was a clue which Lieutenant Hodgson,
commander of the 10th Hussars, was too shrewd an
officer to neglect. He had just brought his regiment
from Perth to be in readiness in case of disturbance,

and here was the very work at hand. Without a
moment's hesitation, therefore, he ordered out a party
of his troops, with which, augmented by a number
of the Kilsyth Yeomanry, he galloped in search of
the rebels.

Meanwhile, the Radicals were on the look-out
for the other patriotic corps which were to join them
at Bonnybridge. None, however, were in sight.
They were growing anxious, and the commanders
frequently scanned the roads leading from the west.
But no host appeared. Neither did any come from
the east. Perhaps it was too soon to expect them.
Was it possible that they could have mistaken the
road? Hardly. Something worse was possible.
They might have been intercepted and taken prisoners. The party who were to come by Kirkintilloch and Kilsyth would certainly be in danger of
capture, unless warned in time as to the presence of
soldiers on the route. All, indeed, might be right;
but it began to dawn upon Alan and the two generals
that some parts of the arrangements had miscarried,
from whatever cause.

From the canal bank Baird signalled Hardie to
join him with his men, which was at once done. A
council of war was held, during which very strong
opinions were expressed as to the remissness of their
expected allies.

While the graver heads were thus joined together

in solid discussion, two of the youngest patriots, Andrew White and Willie Tait, who were mere lads, laid down their pikes, and enjoyed themselves by having a friendly game at marbles — if the word marbles can be applied to the leaden bullets which they used for the purpose.

The decision come to by the council was so far wise. It was resolved that the band of liberators should make no further advance until they obtained some definite intelligence either from the east or from the west. Scouts were about to be dispatched in both directions, when King was seen approaching rapidly from the direction of Camelon.

Baird, Hardie, and Dalziel demanded energetically how it was that the promised auxiliaries had not arrived? King could not tell, and he appeared himself astonished and indignant that the forces from the west had delayed so long. He still believed, however, that they would come; and in the mean time, the Camelon company was preparing, and would join them in less than an hour. When informed about the hussar who had passed to Kilsyth; King said,

'It was a mistake to let him pass. You should either have turned him back or taken his horse and arms, so as to delay him as long as possible from joining his regiment. By this time they will know of our whereabouts, and I suspect they will be upon

us immediately.   Look here,' he added, after a moment's reflection; 'while I go back to hasten the
Camelon corps, it will be as well for you, Baird, to
lead your men over the brow of Bonnymuir, so as to
be out of sight, and I shall guide the Camelonians
towards the rear of your position.   Steady — and
quick!'

As King darted away, Baird and Hardie led their
men to the south side of the canal, which they reached
by a subterranean viaduct; and in less than a quarter
of an hour the Radicals were couched among the
spring heather, glad to be at rest, after their long
and fruitless march.

The weather had partially cleared up; and although the heath was not quite dry, still it was fresh,
sweet-smelling, and altogether pleasant.   Several of
the men fell soundly asleep at once.   Others soothed
themselves by ascending into the region of day-
dreams upon clouds of tobacco smoke; while some,
more martially inclined, burnished the rust from
their muskets.

Baird, Hardie, and Dalziel, after making arrangements against surprise, met as by mutual consent,
and looked into each other's faces, where the same
thought seemed predominant.   Apart from the main
body of the Radicals, they sat upon a knoll which
was rich with budding heather-bells.   Sitting with
their faces to the north, they saw the bristling range

of the Ochils, touched with gray mist upon the upper
scalps, and seamed with little streamlets, which glittered like silvery threads.   Farther to the north, the
more magnificent Grampians muffled themselves behind an awful curtain of clouds, and only now and
then revealed a snowy shoulder through some windy
rent.   Away to their right, the three Radicals saw
the rocky bulk of Stirling Castle, which they were to
have taken that night; and at the same moment their
eye caught the grand summit of the Abbey Craig,
beyond which the river Forth flowed towards the sea
in many a gleaming convolution.   In spite of the
peculiar fix in which they found themselves, these
three young fellows were struck with the beauty and
grandeur of the scene.

Only for a moment, however; for their eyes, having scanned the panorama, once more turned significantly upon each other.   Alan spoke first.

'I think, gentlemen, that we had better be plain
with each other.   My opinion is that this business
is a failure, and that we should give it up in the
mean time, and endeavour to get those fellows safely
back to their homes.   What say you?'

'Since ye hae spoken first, Dalziel,' Baird replied
with evident relief, 'I may admit that the same
thought has been in my mind for the last hour or
mair.   It's a hard thing to say, but I doubt it's true.
What's your idea, Hardie?'

'To judge frae appearances, it's no possible to come to ony ither conclusion. What way it has failed I canna comprehend. Last nicht, and even this morning, everything seemed possible. Now, I confess, there's naething for't but to trudge hame— though, for mysel', I'm gae sweer't to gang back to Glasgow sae ingloriously. It's waur than a defeat. They'll laugh at us. If we had only a wound to show—the want o' an arm or something—there wad be some pleasure as weel as glory in gaun back to St. Mungo's. There's something shamefu' in sic a failure.'

'You have anticipated me, Hardie,' said Alan, 'in your feeling about going back to the city. I fear I can't go back at all.' And as he spoke, hé became very thoughtful, and began to pluck heather-bells abstractedly, like one whose mind is intensely preoccupied. Then he roused himself a little, and added, 'There is a lady in Glasgow, one whom—that is— Why shouldn't I tell you? She is one I love; and I have sacrificed her for this. On this subject we quarrelled and parted; and here I am, in the very position she predicted. It is singular how some women foresee things.'

Baird turned away his face with much emotion, for he was in a position similar to that of Alan. It remained for Hardie to speak.

'Mr. Dalziel, ye've put a pike richt through my

heart by what you say. I hae a sweetheart too—as bonnie and kind a lass as e'er ye saw atween the een. It was wi' a sair faught I managed to get awa frae her arms. Gudeness, how she clung to me! I thought she wad hae broken her heart. At last she let me ago, and looking at me wi' a face like a ghost, she said solemnly, "Andrew, ye'll ne'er come back!" It was sheer fricht. Weel, I micht gang back; but I dinna like, after this shamefu' end. I think I'll gang out o' the road for a month or twa, till the storm blaws by.'

'It's queer,' said Baird, in a husky voice, ' that we three should be in the same pickle. There's something no canny in't; and ye mind what auld Elsie Peden said?'

'Come, Baird,' Alan remarked hastily, ' you must not think about the fancies of that old creature. Do you know she told me to go home, but that I must ride for it. When I told her that I had neither horse nor home, she took hold of my hand in the manner of the fortune-tellers, looked into my face, and said that I had a home which I had never seen, and that a swift horse aye comes to the gallant rider. I wish it would come now.'

'I never kent Elsie to be wrang.'

'Richt or wrang, Baird,' Hardie said, 'I propose that we remain here till gloaming comes on, and then march back the way we cam'.'

The other two assenting, they were in the act of loading their tobacco-pipes, when Baird, starting to his feet, cried hurriedly,

'There's Lattimer's whistle!'

'Wait!' said Hardie.

Again the whistle blew.

'Wait!' repeated Alan.

Yet once more blew the whistle, and louder than ever.

'To arms!' shouted all three in unison; 'the troops are upon us!'

'To arms!'

'To arms!'

The call was thus taken up by the Radicals lying among the heather, as they started to their feet, grasping their pikes and guns. Baird, Hardie, and Dalziel ran to the brow of the slight elevation on the south side of which they had been sitting, and at once perceived what they knew was meant by the signal-whistle.

Some thirty troopers were marching upon them. There could be no mistake about it. The living fact stared them in the face. Yonder were the proud horses, their necks clothed with thunder, pawing the moor, coming to meet the armed men, and smelling the battle not very far off. Rock-like, on the horses, sat the stern troopers, their sabres jingling at their sides, and their helmets gleaming in the sun.

'Now then,' said Alan briskly, yet seriously, 'here come your scar-makers. You can hardly escape without a mark of glory.'

'Are ye a guid rider, Alan?' Hardie answered interrogatively, as he looked at the advancing troop.

'Only give me a horse, and you'll see.'

'See, yonder it comes—as sure as death—a horse without a rider—the very animal that Elsie tell't ye to mount.'

Alan turned pale as he replied, 'Then, by Jove, I'll try it, if you won't consider it cowardice to escape.'

'Not a bit,' his companions replied. 'Try it, by a' means, and God be wi' ye.'

'Let us three shake hauns,' said Baird with feeling, but very steadily; 'I and Hardie may never see ye again, Alan; but if ye manage to escape, and we be ta'en, dinna forget us.'

'Never! But don't talk about being taken, man. Let us have a blow at them.'

'We'll no be ta'en without a blow, I'll warrant ye. Now, then, men! All ready?'

A shout was the response.

'Forward! Forward!'

Baird's plan of battle was simple. A dry-stone dyke extended along the moor, right across the path of the Hussars, and of this fortunate barrier the Radical leader at once took possession, and planted

his men behind it. One little gap he filled with
four pikemen, and then gave his orders. They were
to reserve their fire until the soldiers were at close
quarters, to fire low, and to keep cool and steady.

Meanwhile the Hussars, making a slight detour,
came under the shelter of a clump of trees, from
which they fired a shot or two in the air, for the
purpose evidently of frightening the Radicals into
surrender. Hearing the shots without feeling any
of the bullets, the patriots stuck behind their dyke
bravely, awaiting the further approach of the enemy.
Lieutenant Hodgson, supported by detachments of
the Kilsyth Yeomanry, under the command of Lieutenant Davidson, then led his men forward. Their
first effort was naturally directed against the gap in
the dyke, which was held by the Radical pikemen.
Before permitting the attack, however, the officer
advanced to the front and shouted at the top of his
voice,

'I call upon you, in the name of the King, to
lay down your arms at once, and surrender to authority.'

'Never!' was the Radical response.

'Then your blood be on your own heads!'

The battle then commenced in earnest, and raged
exactly ten minutes. The Hussars charged the gap
furiously, but were bravely repulsed, with a few skin-
deep pike-scratches. Baird and Hardie stood on

each side of the gap, each with a musket, cheering
and steadying their men. One of the troopers, more
adventurous than the rest, urging his horse close to
the dyke on the right of Hardie, and making a circle
of lightning with his sword, was received with a
daring pike-thrust from one of the Radicals. The
soldier at once laid his sword across his bridle-arm,
and fired a pistol in the face of the heroic pikeman,
who fell to the ground like one dead.

Dalziel, being the doctor, rushed forward and
pulled this first victim from the *mêlée*, to see whether anything could be done with him. Happily the
fellow was only frightened, and Alan left him on the
cool heath to recover his courage.

A second charge was then made by the troops
upon the gap, which they successfully carried. The
whole of the horsemen rushed through and scattered
most of the Radicals right and left. The two leaders,
Alan, and a few others, however, stood their ground
bravely.

Baird, after firing at, but fortunately missing,
Lieutenant Hodgson, presented his empty musket
at him and warned him off, or he would fell him to
the ground. The officer fired at Baird, but the
pistol flashed, the bullet not having its billet in that
case. Being pushed on another point, Baird smashed
a private trooper with the butt - end of his piece,
which brought down upon him the sergeant of the

Hussars, who fired without effect. Baird then attacked the sergeant with great fury, and, before the latter could draw his sword, wounded him in the right arm and the side. In other parts of the field there was a good deal of slashing and battering. One Radical jaw was laid completely bare, which destroyed for ever the rhetorical faculty of its owner. Another patriot was left for dead on the moor, but he survived and escaped. Two or three hand-to-hand encounters which fell to Hardie's lot were productive only of a few shallow bruises. Alan saved a patriot's life. A hussar had ridden the fellow down, and was about to finish him with his sword, when the gallant doctor neatly shattered the assailant's right hand with a pistol shot, and made the sword drop from his hand. It must be said of Lieutenant Hodgson, that he prevented more blows than he dealt. He was eager to avert bloodshed, and defended the Radicals against the fury of his own men, receiving as his reward a badly lacerated hand. At length, however, in obedience to the repeated calls of this generous officer, the patriots surrendered; though some of them, who flung down their weapons and fled into the neighbouring wood, were pursued by the Yeomanry.

At this point occurred one of the most striking incidents of the fight. Alan had not forgotten the fact of the riderless horse. It appeared that the

yeoman to whom this animal belonged had fallen
down in a fit at the edge of the moor, and was carried back to a roadside cottage. But his comrade,
refusing to leave the horse with the same people,
had taken it along with him. Now, when the battle
was over, and the pursuit of the flying Radicals
began, the yeoman who had charge of the vacant
steed, being eager to show his skill in the hunting
of men, and having more faith than wit, flung the
reins to Alan in passing, and told him to hold it
until he returned. Baird and Hardie, who saw this
curious fulfilment of Elsie's apparently mad declaration that the swift steed always comes to the good
rider, gave Alan one glance of intelligence.

This was enough.

Alan rose to the saddle at a single bound, and,
waving a swift farewell to his comrades, galloped
at lightning speed from the field, amid a shower of
Radical cheers and trooper bullets. One or two of
the latter whistled ominously at his ear, and three
hussars were sent after him; but they might as well
have tried to catch the wind as catch him, flying for
his life on the airy back of a semi-Arabian mare,
who felt the commanding touch of a master.

He was away, and they could not, and would
never, overtake him. But whither should he ride?

Whither? Whither?

These were the questions which kept singing in

his ear as he rushed over moss and moor. Instinctively, however, he aimed steadily at the south; and when at length he caught a southward-going road, the winged creature, like the war-horse in Job, swallowed the ground with fierceness and rage, as if he smelt the battle afar off, and heard the thunder of the captains, and the shouting.

As for the remaining Radicals, they were gathered together, and marched or taken in carts as prisoners to Stirling Castle—that very fortress which they had hoped to make the first of a glorious series of captures in the cause of right and freedom.

CHAPTER XXIII.

CLOSING IN.

DR. BANNATYNE, then the most skilful physician in Glasgow, after a careful study of the case of Lady Carmyle, assured his lordship that the afflicted lady would speedily recover from her mental disturbance, but that, probably in the course of a year or two, she would slowly decline and die. The length of her life would, however, depend on certain conditions. When his lordship asked what these conditions were, the doctor replied,

'They are very simple. After giving her a few

months' repose, you must travel with her ladyship. She has been much accustomed to travelling; and, strange as it may seem, my lord, it is mainly due to that fact that her general health has been so well maintained. Besides, she has not been subjected to any rougher usage than what is involved in a wandering life. Under more refined circumstances, she could not, I fear, have lived nearly so long, probably not a third of the time she has been absent. Your aim must, therefore, be to make as little difference in her way of life as you possibly can for a couple of years. Take her to Italy, my lord, and, as much as is practicable, make the sky your roof, and don't be afraid of pedestrianism. In the mean time,' the doctor added, 'endeavour to find her late companion, Swallow—or Nelly, as her ladyship calls her. Whether she be able to give you any special information about the history of this wonderful adventure, her influence will unquestionably facilitate the recovery of Lady Carmyle.'

· Lord Carmyle pondered these opinions, felt their reasonableness, and afterwards acted upon them with much success.

The doctor was right. His patient recovered more speedily than even he anticipated. The reason of this is known to the reader. The poor wanderer had nearly recovered before she reappeared to her husband; and the shock of the mutual recognition

only produced a temporary relapse. To his lordship
and the doctor she necessarily appeared to be worse
than she really was. Up till Tuesday, however, her
excitement was still great, and, to her husband, won-
derfully distressing. But on Tuesday afternoon Dr.
Bannatyne succeeded in giving his patient the blessing of long sleep; so that by Wednesday, when she
awoke, she was comparatively calm.

Lord Carmyle remained by her bedside while she
slept, and was present when she opened her eyes.
How ceaselessly and tenderly he had watched her
during this protracted slumber! Scarcely for an instant did he move from her pillow, but sat by her and
hovered about her with feelings of indescribable fond-
ness and anxiety, living upon the sweetness of her
pallid face. Her beautiful brown hair was faintly
sprinkled with silver; but in repose her features did
not appear to be so greatly altered from the loveliness of youth as might have been expected. Not a
single wrinkle was to be seen; though now and then,
when some vision passed before her mind, her brows
would contract into an expression of fear which was
painful to behold. When she smiled, however, as
sometimes she would do, no face could be more
peacefully seraphic. Once she all but wakened, and
began to speak. Her husband stooped towards her,
and listened intently, and heard her whisper, in swift
broken syllables:

'Are you sure, Nelly, that they are living? Shall we see them? O, my poor husband!—my dear baby! Come away, Swallow! Come, come! Hawk is following! Come!'

These words roused in Lord Carmyle feelings of deep grief and indignation. They proved the indestructible affection of Margaret; and they revealed a glimpse of the wrong of which she and himself had been the victims. At another time, towards morning, she clasped her hands together, and sang, or rather sobbed, in a low sad voice, liquid snatches of an old pathetic ballad—one of those which his lordship remembered so well, and the hearing of which once more, under such peculiar circumstances, quite unmanned and melted him.

'O, my poor wife,' he whispered, 'what a wasted life ours has been!'

The weary hours passed on—the weary weltering hours; for it was a night of rain-storm—the same night upon which the Radicals assembled at Germiston and marched away upon their fatal errand. As his lordship sat by his slumbering wife, he heard the rain washing without, and the flooded river plunging through its gorge under the walls of the castle.

Day dawned drearily; but still Lady Carmyle slept on; and still her husband sat patiently by her pillow, gazing anxiously upon her serious and thoughtful face. As the hours advanced, she grew

restless, and her countenance became slowly illumined with the light of waking intelligence—as the
pale face of dawn becomes filled with the clear light
of day. His lordship watched with a strained intensity the opening of his wife's eyes. When she at
length awoke, Dr. Bannatyne's hopeful predictions as
to the probable immediate effects of sleep, which was
also repose, were fairly fulfilled. After a short in-
terval of confusion and surprise, Lady Carmyle became calm and collected beyond all anticipation.

The doctor, though endeavouring to be grave and
cool, was nevertheless visibly jubilant; and Lord Carmyle was, in consequence, elated and happy. They
were, however, slightly startled by the first words
uttered by Lady Carmyle, who asked, with some
energy:

'Have you found her?' meaning by that her late
companion Swallow.

Divining what she meant, his lordship answered,
soothingly yet hesitatingly:

'No, my dear; at least, we have not heard from
Mr. Archer; but I think we may rest assured that he
will succeed, if success is possible at all, in saving
Nelly from—from any danger to which she might be
exposed. I expected a message from Hamilton this
morning; and it may arrive any moment.'

Her ladyship was silent, and looked disappointed.
The doctor said:

'I have all faith in Archer; and knowing something of the measures he has adopted, it seems impossible that anybody can escape that ought to be taken. There can be little doubt about that. If I have any doubt, it is perhaps about Nelly. I sincerely hope that she may be able to render some help. She may be able—indeed, I think she will; yet I would caution your ladyship—Nelly may not remember. It may be well, at least, not to expect too much from the poor creature.'

'Poor Nelly! poor dear Swallow!' Her ladyship looked wistfully at her husband for a moment, and then at the doctor, as she added, putting her hand to her brow: 'You are perhaps right, doctor. I feel confused still, and everything seems so misty and dreamlike, and so far away. Yet, amid all the confusion, two things have ever been clear to me. She told me that, with God's help, I should again see true friends—friends that never were false.'

'And so you have, Margaret, so you have;' and as he spoke her husband took her hand, looking fondly into her eyes, which seemed burdened with the mist that she was trying to penetrate. She brightened in responding:

'Ah, James, I have found *you* true and brave, and not false, as I was told! It was cruel of Sir John to say it—cruel, cruel! But Nelly also told me that I should see our baby. O, if it should be true!

if it should be true! Tell me, James, is it true?
May I believe it?'

'My dear Margaret, nothing is impossible; but
this is to me only a hope—I have no knowledge.
We can hope, if we cannot believe. Wait till Nelly
comes.'

Lord Carmyle hardly knew what he said. He
could not conscientiously hope that Nelly's assur-
ance, or rather Lady Carmyle's delusion, as he believed it to be, would or could possibly come true.
Happily the doctor ended this conversation with
some dexterity, contriving as he did, without com-
mitting himself, to leave upon her ladyship's mind
the impression that there were good grounds for
hope. Not long after this the expected message
from Archer arrived. It was brief, but pregnant:

'We have them! This morning, shortly after
midnight, my faithful iron-handed scouts pounced
upon Hawk as he was leaving the Hermitage, taking
Swallow with him. The struggle was frightful; but
one giant was no match for two; so he was compelled
to yield. We have him safe; and, in accordance
with your wish, I shall bring him before yourself
some time in the afternoon. From Nelly I have
learned a fact at the truth of which I have myself
for some time guessed, but dared not hint from want
of direct evidence. You shall hear it from the lips

of the witnesses. Prepare to be astonished. Further, to confirm my suspicions, Sir John Home is to-day *non est*. It appears that, hearing the struggle with Hawk, he came out to see what was the matter, and, seeing, vanished like a guilty thing away. Whither he has fled no one knows; but the long sure Arm will find him in the uttermost parts of the earth.

'A new trouble has come upon me. I have to-day a mad letter from my friend Dalziel, who seems to have joined himself fatally with these wretched Glasgow Radicals. The fools! If *he* were not with them, I could curse them! Should evil befall him, I herewith bespeak your good offices in his favour. Indeed, my lord, you must befriend him. Did he not once help to save your life? You must now help to save his; for, if I mistake not, it is in imminent jeopardy. Pardon this language; but he is my friend; and as he has been yours in a vital sense, you will, I am sure, be not less vitally his.'

Some points in this letter puzzled Lord Carmyle; and he was trying to catch the meaning of them, when two visitors were announced—visitors the presence of whom, at this particular juncture, puzzled him more than even Archer's epistle. However, his lordship went to them at once, and was evidently pleased to see them.

'My dear Miss Walkingshaw! and Christine the

fairy, more fairy-like than ever !—sincerely welcome !
Ah, my dear, do you remember taking me for your
father ? That was a pleasant illusion ; but how much
more pleasant it would be to me, were I really your
father, and you my daughter ! What a queen you
would make !' And his lordship took her kindly by
the hand, and gazed with admiring tenderness in the
face of the blushing girl. 'Can I serve you, my
dear ?' he added. 'Speak, and command me ! Your
father, is he—'

'You must pardon us, my lord,' said Miss Walkingshaw, 'for this intrusion at such a time. Mr.
Dundas is well, and we come here wholly against his
will.'

'It is my fault, my lord,' interposed Christine,
eager to take all blame upon herself.

'Then it is pardoned. A fault that brings you
to Carmyle is a virtue. When I visited your house,
for the purpose of seeing a certain gallant yet foolish
friend of ours, you may remember that I went unin-
vited and unexpected.'

'That foolish friend, my lord,' Miss Walkingshaw broke in, 'is more foolish than ever, and in
connection with the same folly. It is about him that
we come to consult your lordship. He has gone off
with the Radicals on some criminal expedition.'

'The madman ! He can't escape. The Government are determined to make examples this time ;

and they will select the most conspicuous persons. How desperately foolish! Was there no person to prevent him? Last time, his father's death saved him; but we can't expect wise men to die every day to save fools.'

'I tried to save him, my lord,' said Christine; 'but he would not listen.'

'Would not listen to you! Then he deserves to perish! How utterly blind he must have been! Seldom does a man look so rational, and act so madly.'

'O, my lord, save him if you can!' Christine murmured appealingly, and looking into his lordship's face.

'I would fain do so, my dear. I owe Alan a debt of life, and I should like to repay it with interest— but how to do it? I shall be only able, I fear, to soften the blow, not to arrest the arm of justice. But rest assured that nothing which can be honestly done to save the life of this rash, headstrong hero will be neglected by me. Stay a moment,' added his lordship, listening; 'I hear the clatter of a horse. That must be Archer, whom I expected from Hamilton. He is a friend to Alan, and I shall consult him about the affair. He is a wise lad.'

His lordship went to the window of the room, which commanded a portion of the avenue running between the castle and the main road. So soon as

the horseman came in sight, Lord Carmyle exclaimed,

'That is not Archer? Look, Miss Walkingshaw!'

The two ladies at once ran to the window, and
Christine cried joyously,

·'That is Alan! Alan! Alan! He is safe! O!—'

Lord Carmyle caught the girl in his arms, as she
staggered from the window, overwhelmed with excitement. Placing her upon a couch, where she soon
recovered, he whispered,

'You must be bold, my dear lady, and leave me
to deal with the runagate. I shall punish him so
effectually, that he will never again rebel against your
lightest decree.' Then, after a moment's thought,
he added: 'Both of you sit behind this screen, and
neither speak nor move till I call upon you by stamp-
ing my foot. I shall bring Alan hither. Quick, and
keep silence.'

In two minutes his lordship and Alan entered the
apartment, when the latter at once began, excitedly
enough,

'My lord, I come to you in my hour of sorest
need to seek your help.'

'Well, Alan, what is it?'

'Five years ago, my lord, under peculiar circumstances, you said to me, "I owe you a life;" and you
told me to remember the fact. To-day I have cause

to remember it. I have been upon an enterprise of
life and death. It has failed, therefore death is its
reward. For the present I have escaped; but unless
you can afford me the means of concealment until I
contrive to leave the country, I am a dead man!'

'What stupendous folly has brought you to this
pass?'

'My lord, it has sprung from Radicalism; and
while some men praise it as duty, others denounce it
as treason. Whatever I may have called it hitherto,
the folly of it is clear enough to me now.'

'Treason! and you wish me to conceal you from
justice! Do you know, sir, that whoever conceals a
traitor is himself a traitor, and endangers his own
neck? Is it fair to ask me to put my own life in
jeopardy?'

Alan stood confounded for a moment, and then
said, quietly and earnestly,

'Pardon me, my lord; I did not view the matter
in that light. I would not for the world do anything
to compromise you—no, not for a moment. And
after all, what does it matter to me—hopeless, home-
less, and friendless? Farewell, my lord.'

'Stay, sir. I don't think I should be justified
in allowing you to escape; and now, when I think
on't, I won't let you go. You know that I am a
magistrate of the county, and have power to arrest
all—'

' Surely, my lord, you cannot—'

' Can't I, sir ? I am resolved to punish you with a rigour beyond your own imagining.'

' As you please, then,' said Alan, in a tone of weariness and indifference, as he flung himself into a seat, with his back fortunately to the screen ; ' my treason is not my worst sin.'

' No, indeed ; it is not. You have done worse. Like a fool, you have despised the wisdom of the purest and loveliest lady in Christendom—an all but unpardonable sin. But you will sin no more against that divinity, I'll warrant. I shall bind you in chains that you never will break, though you were ten times a giant.'

' So be it, my lord. Do your worst.'

' So be it, then ;' and his lordship stamped his foot, as if summoning some attendant. Christine glided from behind the screen, and at a sign from the magician, crept noiselessly behind Alan, and clasped his head in her arms, whispering,

' Alan !—O, Alan !'

' Bind the traitor ! Hold him relentlessly in those chains of alabaster, and there let him be a prisoner for life ! That is my sentence. It is irrevocable !'

' Christine !' cried Alan, starting up amazed.

' Ay, Alan,' said Lord Carmyle, ' it is Christine. You can't find her equal. It is thus I punish you ;

and if you are willing to bind yourself to her and to me to keep the peace for life, I shall help to conceal you for a month or two—not otherwise.'

'I swear, my lord. I repent of all my past sins and offences.'

'Who would not repent, with such a piece of loveliness for a prize? My surprise is that you ever sinned. But seriously, Alan, I was sorry at seeing you commit such a fatal error; and now you add to my own happiness by your repentance. Miss Walkingshaw and I are witnesses to your oath, and to this reconciliation.'

'I shall answer for Christine,' said Miss Walkingshaw.

'And I for Alan,' his lordship rejoined; 'and so far, this affair is settled. Stay here till I return. I have some business with Archer, who, I hear, has just arrived.'

CHAPTER XXIV.

AT LENGTH.

WHEN Lord Carmyle met Archer, he told him that Alan and Christine had arrived at the Castle, and under what conditions; and the young lawyer

assured his lordship that nothing could be better
timed.

'This business, I may as well inform you, my
lord, slightly concerns Alan. I believe that both
Hawk and Swallow know a fact or two in which my
friend has some material interest.'

'Be quick, then. Have you brought them with
you?'

'All, except one, whom I expect immediately. I
wish you to concede one thing.'

'Well.'

'Let Alan, at least, if not Christine and Miss
Walkingshaw, be present with us when you see that
fellow Hawk and Swallow. They have met before.
I expect that the result of the interview will be a
pleasant surprise to Alan, and by no means un-
pleasant to you. Grant this, my lord, and I guar-
antee that you will be satisfied.'

Lord Carmyle was puzzled at the nature of this
request, and paused long before he answered. Knowing, however, that he could rely upon the wisdom and
discretion of Archer, he at length yielded, saying:

'Arrange the matter as you please. Remember,
however, that in this phase of it, I regard you rather
in the light of a friend than merely as a man of
business.'

'Thank you, my lord. You will not repent this
confidence.'

His lordship hastened to Lady Carmyle, whom he found still better—so well, indeed, that she was actually up, and walking about. News of the arrival of Nelly and Hawk had reached her, and she was anxious to learn the result of the investigation which she knew her husband and Archer were about to make. She seemed to be in a state of keen expectancy, which greatly disturbed his lordship, who dreaded the influence of Nelly's communication. Dr. Bannatyne, however, who had resolved to stay over the investigation, and watch the effect of it upon his patient, reassured his lordship.

At length Archer brought the parties face to face.

There stood Hawk, huge and sombre, like a peak in mist, gazing gloomily on the man whom he had helped to wrong so deeply; and glancing at Alan, whom he would have murdered, but for a pathetic jet of music which was sung out of the gulf by Nightingale, who was now under the same roof with him, marvellously restored to the arms of her husband.

Near Hawk stood Swallow, pale and trembling, who had also been an instrument, though unwillingly, in the perpetration of the crime. Hawk was carefully guarded by two men nearly as huge as himself.

Lord Carmyle, grave and thoughtful, scanned the gigantic offender and his slim, pallid companion; but apparently could make nothing of them. On the right of his lordship stood Archer, determined, and with an expression of triumph in his eye. He smiled on Christine, and gave Alan a peculiar glance, which might mean, ' Observe now, my mad Radical, and very sceptical friend, and see whether I have been dreaming of late. If I don't solve the problem of your existence, score me out of your book of friendship, and never trust me more.'

Alan, who, along with Christine and Miss Walkingshaw, stood on the left of Lord Carmyle, responded to Archer's glance by plainly saying with his eyes, ' You are dreaming, my sanguine friend; and your scheme, whatever it is, will topple about your ears like a house built with illusions instead of good bricks, faithful mortar, and honest art. Take warning !'

Christine and Miss Walkingshaw were simply puzzled.

' My lord,' Archer began, ' I have told you that one witness is yet wanting; but we can, nevertheless, go on in the mean time. In order to make the work as brief as possible, I shall divide it into several points. First, I accuse Sir John Home of the sin of falsehood; and, second, of the crime of abduction and conspiracy.'

' Archer, is this true ?'

' Have patience, my lord. I accuse Sir John of the sin of falsehood, inasmuch as, twenty-three years

ago, he propagated against your lordship the lie that
you were faithless to Lady Carmyle. I accuse him
further of the crime of abduction, inasmuch as, at
the same date, he employed the man named Hawk,
now standing before you, to spirit away Lady Carmyle
and her child, with the deliberate purpose of destroy-
ing the Carmyle succession, in order that he himself
or his descendants, being nearest of kin, might enjoy
your lordship's titles and estates. That these pro-
positions are true, I dare aver. They are true, or I
am false! I call Hawk to witness.'

Lord Carmyle sat like one utterly confounded.
It was difficult all at once to believe that his cousin
could be the author of so heartless and so enormous
a crime. At length he spoke, but in a voice quivering and broken. Addressing Hawk, he asked,

'Is this true, sir?'

'True to the letter, my lord. True in every particular.'

Hawk hung his head as he replied.

'And who are you,' his lordship resumed, 'who
could so abuse yourself—who could imperil your immortal soul in so terrible a crime?'

'It matters nothing here, my lord, who I am. It
is enough to say that Sir John Home tempted me
in an evil hour—won me to his purpose. But not
wholly; I did not murder poor Nightingale—I mean
her ladyship—and her child. Bad as I am, and have

been, I could not do that. Besides, it was more profitable to keep them alive.'

'Do you mean us to believe, sir, that our child is still living?'

'Allow me to answer, please,' said Archer with emphasis. 'My next proposition is, my lord, that your son *is* still living, a full-grown, handsome, and heroic young man; and more, that he is at the present within the walls of Carmyle Castle. My lord, in Alan Dalziel behold your son!'

'You mock me, Archer!'

'By Heaven, my lord, I do not! It is true, or everything is false. Let these two bear witness.'

'Yes, my lord,' said Hawk, 'everything else may be false, but that is true.'

'O, my lord,' Swallow repeated, 'it is true—it is true! The bonnie bairn is my lady's son. It was me that gied him into the keeping o' Mrs. Dalziel—the Lord forgie me for the wrong I did to my lady and her wee sweet bairn. But my lady was out o' her mind then wi' grief at her lady mither's death, and wi' the thought that your lordship was fause, and wad never come back to her mair. That was the cruel lee that brak her heart and clean turned her head. But, the Lord be praised!' added Swallow, with a hysteric sob, 'it's a' ended now. The wrang is made richt; the weary Nightingale has got back to her ain warm nest, and the bonnie bairn

to the arms o' his richtfu' parents. O that I could
dee!'

When Archer made his crowning declaration,
Lord Carmyle rose suddenly and stood gazing at
Alan, while Alan, no less astonished and confounded,
stood looking at his lordship. Neither could for the
moment articulate a syllable; but while Hawk and
Swallow were confirming the truth of Archer's statement, the father, keeping his eye fixed upon his son,
was busy wondering whether so startling a revelation would kill or save his poor wife, the true mother
of Alan. Among the whirl of ideas which flashed
through his mind, this—that strong men and women
had often been struck dead by sudden shocks of joy
—kept ominous predominance. His own excess of
joy almost choked him—took from him all power of
speech. If it was so with him, a strong man, what
would it be with Lady Carmyle, weak with long suffering?

His lordship's doubts and fears received an unexpected solution.

Lady Carmyle, unable to quell her passionate
curiosity, had compelled Dr. Bannatyne to assist her
in playing the spy. Under the kindly yet stern eye
of the doctor, she had listened to the great, the overwhelming revelation, without being overwhelmed.
She neither screamed nor fainted; though for several
moments her brain wavered on the thin edge of the

dizzy abyss of unconsciousness. But she did not faint. Recovering while Lord Carmyle and Alan were gazing at each other, she staggered from her concealment, supported by the doctor, and fell into the arms of her husband, crying pathetically:

'O, my dear husband, we are blessed indeed! I have heard all—heard all! Do not fear for me.'

Then, looking with a melting eye at Alan, she stretched her hand to him and cried sobbingly,

'Our son!'

'O, my mother—my father!'

And Alan, shaken with excitement, was clasped by both his parents, as he rushed to them, and knelt by their side.

It need not be told what effect this scene had upon the true hearts there. But we may state that Hawk—the sternest and stoniest soul in the company—shivered from head to foot; and he made the discovery that, as something within him bled at this tender sight, he could not surely be wholly a monster.

As Hawk was marched off between his guards, Archer introduced his last witness—a middle-aged woman, dressed in mourning. When Alan caught sight of her, he advanced hastily, took her by the hand, kissed her cheek, and said,

'Mrs. Dalziel, my dear foster-mother!'

Then he told her briefly what had happened;

and, with tears in her eyes, she addressed Alan's noble parents.

'My dear lord and lady, I thank God I hae lived to see this day! Alan was a blessing to me; and I am sure he will be nae less to you. He was aye good, generous, and brave—maybe a wee thing owre brave; but that's a guid faut, that time'll mend. God bless you, Alan! and bless you too, my dear lady, his true mither! Your sufferings hae been mony and great; but Providence has sweetened the cup at the bottom. Alan,' she said almost sternly, 'as I yield ye to your parents, sae I gie your parents to you; and I charge ye to mak them happy. Ye hae muckle to thank the Lord for. See that ye dinna forget to thank Him; for without His help, Alan, nae fortune can be fortunate, and nae happiness can be happy.'

Mrs. Dalziel, after speaking a few words to Christine and Miss Walkingshaw, was then brought face to face with Swallow, upon whom she looked long in dumb surprise.

'Ay, ay,' she at length said, 'it's you. Ye're gay changed, but I ken ye—ye're the lass that brought me the wee sweet lammie. I was glad ye didna come back to tak Alan awa'. Ye did wrang, nae doubt; but it was joy and comfort to us; sae I canna blame ye for mysel; and I hope God'll forgie ye.'

Swallow could only moan and weep.

Lord Carmyle had been whispering to Lady Margaret, who rose with a happy smile on her face, and went to Christine, whom she took by the hand and led back to her husband. As she did so, she kissed Christine on the brow.

'My dear Christine,' his lordship said, as he took her hand, 'you remember kissing me once by mistake, and calling me father? Since then, how often have I wished that I had such a daughter, and that I were your father! That salute of yours must have been prophetic. You will really become my daughter, will you not? It is not half an hour since I gave Alan and you to each other, before I knew that Alan was my own son. Now that I do know, I give you to each other again. Take her, Alan, and think that Heaven has given you the sweetest lady in the land.'

'O, my lord, you are a generous father!'

'Only just, my good son—only just and safe. I have learned in pain the secret of happiness.'

'Take him, Christine,' said Lady Carmyle. 'Alan will be worthy of you; though I think that you are worthy of the best and the noblest.'

'My sweet mother and noble father,' said Christine, in a low tremulous voice, 'I take Alan, but only to give him back to you along with myself—to live for you, to love you, and to serve you!'

'Amen!' breathed Miss Walkingshaw, with tears

in her eyes; 'this will startle your father, Christine; yet I think it will please him too. You two loved each other long ago, and it seems right that you should do so still. The love that folly could not kill, good fortune ought not to kill. Pardon me, Alan, for saying so.'

'My dear Miss Walkingshaw,' Alan replied, 'you were ever a clear speaker of truth. Be still so, and fear nothing from me. Without yielding my political faith, I can thank you for reproving my political folly—as I thank you for still approving our love, as you did in the past, when I was in the shadow. But we owe all to the goodness of his lordship, my dear father.'

'Not altogether,' said his lordship; 'there stands Archer, without whose shrewdness and skill the work of this day might have been wholly incomplete. He is the magician.'

Archer shook his head in negation, as Mrs. Dalziel remarked solemnly,

'Nae doubt, my lord, we hae a' our virtues as weel as our vices. But the Lord abin is the Lord below; and without the help o' His kindly haun, the wrang wad never be richtit. Let us thank Him, baith first and last!'

The heart of each in that curious meeting beat a silent 'Amen' to these wise and not untimely words.

CHAPTER XXV.

CONCLUSION.

IT is impossible to begin the story of any group of individuals at the beginning, as that would lead the narrator back to the Garden of Eden. And it is equally impossible to continue the story to the proper end, for that would take him through the gates of death into the next world.

As, therefore, the present story has no very definite beginning, the reader must be content with what he may regard as a still more indefinite ending. We have no blue or red lights to burn, as they do at the end of certain powerful dramas. All we can afford to do is to append a few hints, which will help to show the reader that Providence must have had some hand in distributing the apparent punishments and rewards which fell to the lot of some of the persons whose characters we have partially indicated in the record now about to be closed.

* * * * * *

How it came to be believed was a puzzle, but it was believed nevertheless, that Glasgow was to be invaded by a Radical army from Strathaven. The day after Bonnymuir, as a matter of fact, some dozen Radicals marched from that town to the top of Cath-

kin Braes—a low range of hills two miles south-east
of the city—where they planted a flag bearing the
inscription, ‘Scotland free, or a desert.’ They expected to be joined on that commanding position by
thousands of Scottish and English Radicals in arms;
but all the living creatures they saw there were a few
frisking rabbits, who knew nothing of politics or the
miseries of the nation; and, believing at last that
they had either been misled or betrayed, the invaders
broke up their camp and returned to their homes.

James Wilson, the Strathaven ‘statesman,’ had
accompanied the little army as far as Kilbride, a
village eight miles from Glasgow; but, learning
there that Glasgow was in full possession of the
military and that there was no chance of a popular
rising, the veteran thought better of it, and returned
to Strathaven, whither, however, he was tracked and
arrested.   Others of his friends were arrested also,
and tried along with him.

Politically, the immediate result of the ‘Radical
Risings’ was total failure.   The Crown was satisfied
with three victims—Wilson, who was tried and executed at Glasgow; and Baird and Hardie, who were
tried and executed at Stirling.

They died, believing themselves ‘martyrs to the
cause of truth and justice.’

They died—but the cause of Reform, for which
they worked, not wisely, but too well, did not perish.

It prospered year by year; so that to-day the country peacefully enjoys those blessings of good government, peacefully gained, which the martyrs wished to take by force.

A number of the others who were taken prisoners were transported.

* * * * * *

Sir John Home had disappeared, and could nowhere be found. But a week after the day upon which Lord Carmyle discovered his lost heir, a keeper going his rounds in Cadzow Forest observed some of the wild cattle sniffing curiously round a huge hollow oak. The man drove the cattle away, and examined the inside of the tree, where he saw a sight that made him shun that part of the forest ever afterwards. Within the hollow of the oak lay doubled up the body of a dead man, which turned out to be that of the Baronet. The doctors declared that he had been killed by lightning; and the popular belief was that, chased by the demons of terror and remorse, Sir John had fled to the forest, and, overtaken by the tempest which raged upon the night of his disappearance, had taken shelter in the cavity of the tree. There the long bright arm of God had found him, and put an end to his career. The oak stands to this day; and the slit made by the avenging thunderbolt is still visible.

* * * * * *

Richmond, *alias* Captain Batwing, after receiving the wages of his patriotic work, lived many years, and it is said not unprosperously, in the city of London. It is affirmed, however, that he was an unhappy man. In Scotland, and chiefly in Glasgow and the west, his name was, and still is, held in utter abhorrence by the political descendants of the Radicals. He attempted to vindicate his reputation from the attacks of his enemies by legal processes, but he utterly failed. What became of his principal lieutenants in the holy work of countermining the Radical schemes, Heaven only knows. According to one picturesque legend, most of them died ' perpendicular deaths ;' though it may be safely assumed that they gave up the ghost as ' decently horizontal' as most men. The stinging blow and malodorous bath which Andrew Semple got at Germiston brought on a fever, from which, however, he would probably have recovered ; but when he heard of the splendid fortune of his former fellow-clerk, the ' bastard,' as he was too fond of calling Alan, his weakened body and jaundiced brain could not bear the shock. He died.

*   *   *   *   *   *

On the 10th of April 1821, or exactly a year after the events recorded in the preceding chapter, there was a series of brilliant marriage rejoicings on the Carmyle estates.

Alan had been quickly and quietly sent on a course of European travel and study. Lord and Lady Carmyle followed him, after the irrevocable doom of the three Radicals became known—for his lordship, urged by his son and his own noble kindly soul, had moved heaven and earth to save the lives of the poor men; and it was only when he discovered the inexorable spirit of the Government that he could think on going abroad.

In the mean time, the fortunes of Lewis Dundas took a new turn. We have told that he lost every penny which he possessed, but that he emerged from the destruction with honour unsmirched, and owing no man a farthing. He bore his loss nobly, illustrating in his conduct the firm yet amiable stoicism of his opinions, which, without seeming to do so, contained more of the Christian spirit than the severest technicalities of most religious practice. From her father, Christine had inherited the same grand indifference to the glitter of mere monetary success; so that the loss sustained by her father, though grievous to her for his sake, was to herself personally no calamity at all.

But if loss of fortune was not regarded by Mr. Dundas and his daughter as an irreparable injury, the recovery of a portion of it was nevertheless hailed by them with feelings of the profoundest gratitude. Five thousand pounds was a small sum; but it

helped, in however slight a degree, to make Christine
less dependent upon her husband. Not that Sir
Alan Douglas wanted anything with the unpurchas-
able loveliness of Christine, nor that Mr. Dundas
imagined for a moment that his daughter was not in
herself a sufficient treasure for the best nobleman in
the land. But it was a great comfort to the Laird
to think that Christine was not to be penniless after
all. What charmed him vastly was the wise and
noble manner in which Lord Carmyle had instantly
recognised 'the legislative will of nature in the love
of the two children. That act,' he said, ' proved his
lordship to be a man as well as a lord — a man
shrewd and farsighted, with a long eye to the welfare
of his race.' For it was a favourite opinion of Lewis,
that the vigour of the aristocratic class could only
be maintained by judicious intermarriage with the
fairest and noblest spirits of the class which, though
technically beneath them, may be their equal in
beauty and brain.

Mr. Dundas and Miss Walkingshaw were married
at Christmas ; and, according to arrangement, they
also, taking Christine with them, made a tour on the
Continent in the following spring. They joined the
Carmyle family at Naples, where they stayed some
time, making excursions to the famous places roundabout.   Journeying together, they came homeward
through France to England, at the beginning of

April, on the 10th of which month Sir Alan Douglas and Christine Dundas were married at London.

It was on that day, as we have said, that a series of brilliant rejoicings in celebration of the marriage took place among the tenantry on the Carmyle estates. Of these demonstrations, we shall only say that their success was due to the admirable arrangements made by William Archer, who became quite famous through the skilful part he played in the Carmyle drama.

On the afternoon of the marriage-day, three men and two women were assembled in the cottage formerly occupied by Sandy Dalziel and his wife and Alan. One of these men was the new occupant, and that occupant was Pate Fox.

Mrs. Dalziel had died in the previous autumn, and died happy, Christine Dundas closing her eyes. The cottage and garden falling to Sir Alan, he, remembering how Pate Fox, along with himself, had helped to save Lord Carmyle's life, and remembering also Pate's many kindly offices to Christine, wrote home empowering Archer to put the twister in possession of the house for the term of his natural life, with a comfortable provision besides. At Pate's death, if he should happen to die, Bob Lintie and his wife were to be the next heirs. This last arrangement was due to the tender relationship which existed between the future Lady Christine and gentle May Lintie. Thus, two of the men assembled in

the cottage were Pate Fox and Bob Lintie. The
third personage was Jamie Campbell, who had been
brought from Dunkeld to occupy a comfortable but
by no means a servile post, at Carmyle Castle. This
change, besides being a favourable one for Jamie and
his wife, led to several very important consequences.
It brought Willie Campbell under the eye of Sir
Alan, who, discovering in the lad the spark of genius,
took him under his care, and procured for him a first-
class education. Moreover, as Lady Christine had
taken charge of her friend May Lintie, the latter and
Willie came so frequently in contact that their intercourse led to a liking, then to a loving, and, in
the end, to a marriage.

The party in the cottage—the gentlemen we have
named, with Mrs. Anne Lintie and Mrs. Mary Campbell—had dined—dined too in a manner which was
a pleasant novelty to them ; and now, after disposing
of various toasts, including that of ' Lord and Lady
Carmyle,' they had reached the great toast of the
day—' Sir Alan Douglas and Lady Christine Dundas
Douglas.' This toast was, of course, intrusted to
Pate Fox, who was the presiding genius on the present occasion.

' Leddies and gentlemen,' said Pate, rising, and
exhibiting some degree of feeling, ' although I hae
spouted a gay wheen speeches in my day, and in
some queer circumstances, baith by sunlicht and

munelicht; and although, as a rule, I hae a steeve
eneugh spirit, and a by-ordinar cheek, yet I dinna
think shame to say that, on this great and trying
occasion, there's something like a wee birdie fluttering at my heart; and I doubt there's something no
canny in my throat;' and Pate clutched his chair, as
if pressing down the emotional flux. 'I say, Bob,'
he continued, almost in a whisper, and looking at
random through the room, 'what's gane wrang wi'
the sun? The room's awfu' dark—open the window.'

'It's quite licht, Pate,' Bob Lintie replied.

'O'd, that's queer—I maun be blin',' and as the
twister spoke he raised his withered hands to his eyes,
and discovered what all the rest had seen, that the
sun was clouded with tears. 'Hoots, toots,' he resumed, a little put out, 'this'll no do. We cam'
here to rejoice, no to greet. It's awhile since thae
auld een o' mine were sae wat; and maybe ye'll
forgie me. But when I think on the hale story o'
Sir Alan and Leddy Christine frae first to last, it's
no easy for me, wha hae kent them sae lang, to keep
my heart in its richt place, and my een frae gaun
a'thegither up into my heid.' (Marks of feeling.)
'We maun be firm though!' and Pate hit the table
with his knuckles, as if frightening away his bird-
like emotions; 'we maun be firm, and do justice to
this toast. If ye werena a' mair or less acquent wi'

Sir Alan and Leddy Christine Douglas, naething wad gie me mair pleasure than to tell ye their story owre again. It's ane that'll no be forgotten in a hurry.' (Hear, hear!) 'After we're a' deid, lips that are no born yet will tell't at the ingle-neuks in the winter nichts, and lovers will tell't to ilk ither in simmer time, when sitting on mossy banks, wi' the bees singing psalms abune them up in the green leafy aisles o' the plane trees. It's a story to ken'le a lowe in the hearts o' the pure and the guid. No, mind ye, that I'm gaun to approve o' every step o' Sir Alan's past conduct. He's been a guid freen to me in gi'en' me this bonnie bit house for life. But I'm no gaun to lie down in the glaur and worship him for a' that —it tak's me a' my time to worship God in my sma', sinfu' way. If it was lawfu', though, for ae human creature to worship anither, it wadna be Sir Alan I wad bow the knee to, but to Sir Alan's better hauf. Gude forgi'e me, but I doubt I've committed the sin o' idolatry in my heart already to bonnie Leddy Christine.' (Approbation from the ladies.) 'But I canna help mysel' when I think on a' that she's done for me. It was a' very weel in it's way for Sir Alan to gie me this bien cottage; but Leddy Christine did far mair than that. She was the means,' and Pate lowered his voice solemnly as he spoke, ' she was the means o' saving my soul frae gaun doun the dreary, dreich road to despair and misery. The first time I

saw her the very licht o' her een gied me a glint o'
better things; and when she cam to see me afore
she gaed awa to the Continent, she was sae perfectly
bonnie and sweet and kind that I fan mysel' in
Heeven when she spak and lookit in my face.' (Hear,
hear, and cheers.) 'Just think what she did. She
took my runkled paws in her ain saft, white, mune-
beams o' hauns, and cuddled them as couthily as if
I had been a bit weanie, or her ain grandfaither;
and, wad ye believe't? the last thing she did, in bidding me fareweel, was to loot cannily doun, and kiss
my dazed and withered brow—O'd !—'

'What's wrang wi' ye, Pate ?'

'Ye may weel speer, Jamie,' Pate answered,
drawing the back of his hand across his eyes.

The company rapped the table, and gave a succession of cheers, to afford Pate time to recover a
little. Looking somewhat confused, he resumed,

'Just a word or twa mair, my freens, and I'll
propose the great toast of the day. Ye'll ablins be
thinking that I hae been praising Leddy Christine
to the neglect o' Sir Alan ?'

'No ae bit,' protested the two women in a breath.

'Weel, I had nae intention to wrang the gallant
bridegroom—though I claim the richt to be clean
daft on the subject o' the bride.' (A laugh.) 'I hae
ca'd Sir Alan " gallant," and I'm no gaun to draw
back the word; but I maun tak' the liberty to add

that, a'though he was aye mair or less gallant and
brave, he was far frae being aye wise.'

'Let that flee stick to the wa', Pate.'

'After awee, Bob. I was gaun to declare my
belief that Sir Alan's foolishness in the Radical times
sprang mair frae the guidness o' his heart than frae
the badness o' his understanding. The warm low of
feeling and the whirling reek o' passion clean blinded
the ee o' his reason. Sir Alan hasna what they ca'
a logical intellect. He has mair heart than heid—
though his heid's no that ill either. If he doesna
mak' a great statesman, he's fit for great things;
and he's ane o' them that great statesmen canna do
without. He'll never want for a word or an argument, and he has the power to set common sense on
fire wi' his twa cawn'les o' een and the het coal that
he keeps aneth his tongue. I doubt Sir Alan will
aye be a kind o' Radical—thanks to his sanguine
nature, and the queer schooling he got in the mansion o' Cockmylane, when Mr. Dundas had nae
thought that he was pouring political lava down the
throat o' a lord's son—though I jalouse that the
young birkie very soon began to cast sheep's een at
the Laird's ewe-lamb, and that, I'm thinking, wad
mak' Lewis's words seem like the politics o' heeven.
But that was in the nature o' things; and when I
think on't, it seems to me quite providential that
the twa cam thegither as they did.' (Hear, hear.)

' They'll mak' a braw—I may say a splendid couple!
The Lord bless them! and gie them health, wealth,
wut, wisdom, and weans!' ('Amen,' from the two
mothers, and a double 'Hear, hear,' from Jamie and
Bob.) 'May they be weel as they do well; and sae
let us drink their health. If they be only hauf as
happy as we wish them, their life will be a heeven
on earth. Now then,' said Pate, raising his voice,
' Sir Alan Douglas and Leddy Christine Dundas
Douglas!'

The toast was honoured with great sincerity and
spirit, the very women joining in with a little wine,
which, along with something stronger, Archer had
sent to Pate for the day of rejoicing.

Other toasts followed, appropriate to the occasion.
Some good old songs were also given, and Bob Lintie
made his fiddle perform melodious miracles. In the
middle of one of these, the door opened and shut
suddenly, and a figure walked right to the fire.

' Swallow!' exclaimed Pate.

' Nelly, if ye please, Mr. Fox. Helen Bothwell is
my name. It was my name at least in happier days.'

' Sae be it still, Nelly,' said Mrs. Lintie kindly.
' Sit down and get something to eat. I hope this is
no the least happy o' your days.'

' Na, na!' she said with emphasis; 'this is a
happy day to me—the happiest I hae had since I
left the bonny bairn in this very cottage, ill woman

that I was;' and she rocked herself in her seat, excited by recollections of the past.

'Ne'er fash your heid wi' that,' Pate urged gently. 'It couldna hae been a'thegither bad, since it's turned out sae weel. The way o' the Almichty is whiles gay roun' about; but it's aye His way for a' that. Whaur hae ye been the day, Nelly?'

'I've been in the forest,' she replied, 'rejoicing wi' the birds. Yon's whaur I like to be. I could sit a' day and a' nicht in Cadzow Castle, and hear the win' sough amang the trees and the Avon sing to me as they did in the auld times. They a' seemed to ken about the marriage—the flowers, the trees, the birds, and the burnie. How joyfu' they were a'! But Hawk clean spoilt them.'

'Hawk! Has the villain come back here, after breaking out o' prison?'

''Deed has he, Mr. Fox; but he's gaun awa for ever.'

'Will he, though? No if I can help it. I'll send the beagles after him.'

'Stop, Mr. Fox,' said Nelly, starting up; 'ye'll no do onything o' the kind. And I'll tell ye a secret: Hawk's my ain brither.'

'Hawk your brither!' and Pate scratched his head, greatly puzzled, and as if trying to recollect something. 'Do you mean to tell me that Hawk is Gavin Bothwell the gemkeeper, wha—'

'Keep your thoom on that, Mr. Fox. It's true what I tell ye. But he's gaun awa to America, and he'll no trouble us again. He's a changed man since I saw him last; and I'll never mair see him in this world—never mair.'

'Weel, weel, Nelly, let him gang. I'll no be the man to distress your heart; ye hae suffered plenty already, Gude kens! Sit down, and mak yoursel' comfortable. This is no a day for auld miseries. Let us look forrit, and try to be happy, if we can.'

'Thank ye, Mr. Fox. I kent ye were ower guid to torture even the sinfu', muckle, maybe, though they deserve punishment.'

'I'm no sae guid, Nelly, as ye think; and we a' need to be forgi'en for mair than we confess.'

Nelly seemed pleased, and sat down at the fire, into which she continued to gaze with a sad thoughtful eye. An occasional smile flitted across her face at certain points of the conversation going on around her; and sometimes she would even put in a word, as if desirous of contributing to the pleasure of the hour. But she did not seem to feel at ease, very likely on account of her peculiar recollections, which must have been stirred to their depths and throughout their strange extent. At last she went away; and it may be mentioned, that while she lived with an old widow in Hamilton, she was in all respects under the charge of the Carmyle family, who ever kept a friendly and kindly eye upon her.

The day wore into night with conversations, song-singing, fiddle-playing, and *wut*-combats, in which even the women flourished a bright sword. Mrs. Anne Lintie and Mrs. Mary Campbell had, no doubt, much cause to be thankful and happy. They had both suffered; but bright weather had dawned upon them at last. The radiant little daughter of the former—the charming May—had been away with Christine on the Continent. She was to be one of the bridesmaids that day in London; and she was afterwards to remain the *protégée* of Lady Christine, until some gallant hero would woo her and win her. Then Willie Campbell was at school, delighting everybody by the rapidity of his progress. What were the secret thoughts of the two mothers regarding the destiny of their children, nobody of course could tell; but it appeared to some observers that they desired (what afterwards occurred) that the young people should come together, and so remain, as man and wife—the character of which circumstance we have already hinted at.

The guests were at length all gone. Pate was alone with himself and his household gods—more comfortable and more honoured than he had ever been before in the whole course of his strange life. After pacing up and down for some time, he took a seat by the fire, and tried to collect his thoughts, as if for the purpose of mastering the situation. It was no easy matter; for the events of this particular day had put his brain in a whirl. His efforts at cool reflection were in vain until he lighted a pipe. As he slowly puffed, the turbulence of his thoughts gradually subsided, and he drifted into the region of articulate monologue, his favourite form of self-communion. Many and curious were the thoughts to which he gave expression—thoughts which cannot be repeated here. Then he grew drowsy, and occasionally slept in his chair. During one of these momentary naps, two beautiful figures—a woman and a young girl—entered the chamber, and advanced towards him, both regarding him with heavenly tenderness. The woman stood over him and kissed his brow, while the girl climbed upon his knee, clasped him round the neck, kissed his cheek, and whispered in his ear:

'My dear brother, we have long been watching you. You have endured many years, but not without bravery and patience. Endure a little more, and you will come to us—perhaps in a year—one brief year; and we shall still watch and wait.'

'Only another year, my son,' said the taller figure; 'be patient and humble, and we shall welcome you yonder;' and the figure pointed upward.

Pate murmured, and clasped the dream-child to

his breast; but even in the act he awoke to find his arms vacant. Starting to his feet, he made towards the door, stretching out his arms, as if trying to arrest the vanishing child.

'It's a dream,' he said excitedly; 'but what a dream! My mither and my sister, and baith sae sweet and bonny and happy like.—In a year!' he said musingly; 'weel, sae be it.' And then he fell into his old habit of addressing himself: 'Ye hae your ain luck, Pate. For a' that ye kent, ye micht hae been cut aff in the clap o' a haun; but ye hae a hale year to put your house in order. See that ye dinna forget, for it'll tak' every minute o' your time to repent o' your sins; and even then, if ye're forgi'en, it'll no be because ye deserve forgiveness, but because ye need it.'

He opened the door, and stood for some time looking into the calm heavens.

'It's guid for you,' he continued, 'that there's somebody up yonder, haudin a' the staurs in the hollow o' His haun. Waes me, but it wad be a sad sicht if we couldna believe that He that made them was aye walking amang them, gi'en' them licht and strength, and beauty and grace, to obey the command o' His love. Pate, ye're a favoured mortal, in being allowed to staun here, below sic a roof o' glory, wi' een to see, a heart to feel, and reason to understaun; when, but for Him, ye micht hae been

nae better than a pickle dirt, a chuckie stane, or only
a taed keekin' at the mune frae below a docken leaf,
wi' nae hope o' a hereafter. It's a pity o' the puir
taeds—though I daursay they ken nae better—.'

After a pause, during which he scanned the
heavens, and listened intently to the soft rippling
of the Avon, which flowed a few yards from where
he stood, Pate turned to go in, but halted in turning,
and said:

' O'd, it's awfu' nicht for beauty; the streamie
itsel' seems to ken't, it sings sae sweetly; so do
the trees, wi' their lowne saft sough; and I jalouse
there's something ado in the garden amang the
flowers, or they wadna send out sic a delightfu'
smell at this time o' the nicht. Maybe the fairies
are afit. The fairies! Pate, ye're daft in the heid.
D'ye no see that a' this beauty abune and sweetness
below are just ae grand proof o' the joy o' earth and
heeven at the marriage o' the bonniest fairy, the best
angel, that ever smiled on your ill-faur't life? That
maun be it. Weel, I wish them mony years o' love
and joy, though I mysel' hae only ae year afore me.
That's what they said.' Pate was harping on his
dream. ' There'll be mony changes though or a year
gang by. The Lord gie *me* grace to change for the
better !'

Pate went in and slept; while over the peaceful
clachan of Millheugh beamed the sliding stars; while

onward rippled and ran the Avon through the budding land to the Clyde; and while the deep-volumed
ship-bearing Clyde swung downward and dashed to
the globe-clasping sea.

THE END.

LONDON:
ROBSON AND SONS, PRINTERS, PANCRAS ROAD, N.W.

CPSIA information can be obtained
at www.ICGtesting.com
Printed in the USA
BVOW06s1437121017
497510BV00012B/51/P

9 781163 276563